OVEREXPLOITED

AN EDITORIAL ON THE OVEREXPLOITATION OF THE AMERICAN CITIZEN

OVEREXPLOITED

AN EDITORIAL ON THE OVEREXPLOITATION OF THE AMERICAN CITIZEN

JOE SMITH

Dorrance Publishing Co
585 Alpha Drive, Suite 103
Pittsburgh, PA 15238
Visit our website at *www.dorrancebookstore.com*

ISBN: 978-1-6470-2261-7
eISBN: 978-1-6470-2874-9

CONTENTS

FOREWORD

This book is about human struggle represented by exploitation. Specifically the exploitation of those considered to be common by others considered to be elite. This type of exploitation is not rare, in fact it is really how humans have formed their societies throughout history. The new exploitation is centered on people who "freely" choose their leaders and then because they do not have the time or lack the knowledge to realize that true and even sinister exploitation(over-exploitation) is taking place they become wallowed in a life that falls short of expectations for themselves and their children. In past societies this over-exploitation spelled the end for the exploiter. In today's western communities world leaders and the elite who support them have become skilled ring masters of controlling society, it's path and the people who live within it. Modern exploitative practices can develop a new peasant class. More sophisticated than the peasant classes of the past yet, every bit as exploited in many ways as the pyramid builders, canal diggers, and empire builders of the ancient world. The history of exploitation and where we are today is what I will try to explore. Hopefully the reader will see what I have witnessed as the new exploitation which all of us find ourselves involved in today.

Walls have often been a part of exploitation. There is something about one society having a barrier against another society that impregnates exploitation. China built a series of walls to form (what we now call the Great Wall). This monument to exploitation shows the iron braided souls of Chinese people when it comes to tasks seemingly impossible for laborers without modern hydraulics or gas powered equipment. This wall did not really benefit the peasants who built it but, they died by the thousands to build it anyway. The building of that wall says a lot about ancient Chinese society and has definitely shaped modern China as well. The problems mainland China has with free thinking Chinese areas like Hong Kong and Taiwan are modern examples to mainland Chinese thinking. The Great Wall is also an example of exploitation in the ancient world. Brutal, simplistic and to the point. Emperors had the power of gods over their people and could get them to do almost anything. A supernatural belief in a "Mandate from Heaven" combined with cultural feelings of universal family ties bond Chinese peasants to performing tasks that often lead to their own bodies being the binding agents used to strengthen the wall. Their individual lives soon forgotten but, the wall their over-exploited sweat and blood produced is still standing today.

A different kind of wall exploitation found in history is the stone wall sitting in front of the Union Army at the battle of Gettysburg on the third day of that battle July 3rd 1863. The troops ready to charge that wall were (for the most part) poor white southerners who would benefit very little from victory over the north but, literally charged into the gates of human created hell to benefit the elites who led them. The wave of humanity that lapped against those rocks with a sea of blood was of a poor white class who's only benefit in a slave society was that they were not literally a slave. Many of these people went to battle to defeat those who would take that status from them and believed their deaths were worth keeping others in bondage. Trying to understand this seemingly confused reasoning is rationally hard for most modern thinking people. The reasoning is intertwined in the exploitative process so successfully used by the slave holding class of the South. A true minority elite of the southern population that convinced vast numbers of their fellow non-slave holding brethren that to fight and die for slavery was a great and noble cause. Southern leaders took advantage of ingrained cultural beliefs that combined with their subtle twisting of logic made it seem perfectly normal for a slave-less yo-men farmer to fight like a demon for the right to keep and own slaves. With the exception of German soldiers in WWII, no other group of people have fought so bravely for such an awful outcome as those soldiers charging that wall to give victory to the southern cause. It is one of the great examples of over- exploitation of supposed "free people " one can draw on in history.

The third wall is the border wall promised by Donald Trump in the 2016 presidential campaign. A campaign he won with the promise to the working class that he alone would " Make America Great Again".This unfinished wall and all that it implies has motivated working class people to support a man who would have no idea what paycheck to paycheck existence was like or feel any sympathy for them if their meager incomes were to disappear. This book will attempt to explore how people who have very little to gain in supporting an elite demigod will mark the ballot to do just that very thing.

The ways elites can get "common people" to do their bidding has changed over time. In China the emperors who built the Great Wall used a combination of cultural control, physical force, and propaganda, (fear of the barbarians) to get Chinese peasants to protect their dynasties. The same was done to build the pyramids of Egypt and the great structures found in Mesoamerica. Then you have the Greeks and Romans who used slave labor to build cities , roads, harbors, and other infrastructures that are the marvels of their time and ours. Yet, the common link to all of them is exploitation.

To exploit slaves seems pretty straight forward. The Romans (and to a lesser degree the Greeks) figured out that human capital made warfare payoff. Roman conquest meant slave labor that changed Rome into a slave society. Not based on racism toward the enslaved but, toward their dominance on the battlefield. However, many of the failings of slave societies based on racial superiority were found in Rome as well. Roman accomplishments seem incredible until you realize they created stable conditions in the ancient world for 500 years under the Pax Romana (or Roman Peace). Why did they not develop steam power and rail lines that could have made them so dominant they may have survived to today. The answer most people have is slavery. Instead of using scientific problem solving to create labor saving devices, Romans simply threw more slaves at their problems. Why use your brains when you can use the brawn of other people. In a way the Romans were a victim of their own exploitation.

In the antebellum south the exploitation matured into a racial belief in superiority of one category of people over another. This added to the exploitation by considering the manual property as somewhere between an animal and a human being. For both Romans and Greeks they could not come to racial conclusions because in many cases some of the slaves were Roman and Greek people themselves. The complex paternalism that formed in the antebellum South may unwind the hypocrisy of southerners toward their system and the long time complacency of Northern States toward their sister states in the South. Raping, beating, killing, torturing and throwing away lives of black people was all part of the system. Killing was limited due to the value of a slave. However ,these same masters, who saw their slaves as inferior, would have children with them, allow them into their homes and even rely on them so completely that they could not live without them. The exploitation included the idea that the slave was really better off with the master in control.

In fact I have heard that same sentiment reflected in today's' world . Cliven Bundy (a Nevada Rancher that led the Bundy Standoff) said to reporters," I wonder if the negro wasn't better off as a slave". His reasoning for this outrageous idea was that he felt they were better off picking cotton than they were on government subsidies. Bundy's beliefs are farther than most exploiters of black people will go today. Yet, the stop and frisk policies in New York, the exposed purposeful ticketing of African Americans in Fergusen Missouri, and all the statistics in education, wages, and quality of life in these United States for people of color verse whites, speak the same sorted message as Mr. Bundy. Better off as slaves. Better off exploited to the point where life itself was made pointless. No matter how hard or how well one worked no improvement could be achieved, nothing to look forward to but the same work day after day week after week year after year. An endless treadmill existence that led to a cultural damage seen by Cliven Bundy today who cannot empathetic ally see how an exploited category of people will not recover from such treatment anytime soon. Mr. Bundy cannot see his own privilege that has led to a life of land ownership and relative wealth. To him his hard work and God's grace has made him the man he is today. This type of superiority is more evil than the Chinese emperors or the Greeks and Romans. This type of superiority has a deeper poison to it that still lives in the veins of our society . I will argue it has jumped the race line and can be found between the wealthy elites in our system and the so thought of "common people" of our nation. The wealthy have found a way to exploit the peasant class (white and black) while allowing them to vote and feel they have a say in what goes on, when really it is an illusion. Creating a society without the harshness of the antebellum South or the bluntness of a Chinese Emperor yet, with many of the exploitation s found in both. This book will try to answer why the exploited in today's world allow the over- exploitation.

CHAPTER 1

THE ICU

Death waited quietly in the ICU room as my mother busily fought against the continual slide toward an unplanned end. She hung in a balancing act that the doctors described as a low flying airplane that could easily crash into the ground. Death was there. Waiting for that one miscue. That one mistake that will turn the victim downward toward the end. No more living. No more taking for granted life, time, and people. I did not want to believe it but, again the doctors told me when someone ends up in an ICU they probably did not plan to be there. Something awful happened to them in such a serious way that life hangs in the balance. The chances for reckoning with life and what one has done are not allowed. Focusing on trying to live can cut the time on preparing to die. As one doctor told me, "such is life in the ICU".

For my mother that life threatening event was a surgical procedure that went wrong. A surgeon who cut too deeply in repairing her leg, hit an artery that bled out her life force and caused her to die a very painful death. My brother and I watched this horror play out in a small hospital room helplessly sitting like two centenarians guarding an already doomed comrade. My mother was not willing to die easily. Yet, in the end life left her in such a way she was not able to say goodbye to her eldest son. A regret I believe both of us have.

My mother was a "common person". She lived a life which in many ways was not fair to her or her efforts. She had developed an intense work ethic from her father and worked long past normal retirement age. Her talents and hard work were not often rewarded with payment or recognition by the people and places she worked. She complained about this situation at times but, had within the complaint the underlying attitude that this was the way things were for everybody. Meaning she knew a lot of other people in the same boat as her. She was being over-exploited. She was smart enough to know it. Yet, like many people around her she saw no real way to do anything about it.

Over-exploitation has existed in many societies of the past. The key factor is that these societies are in the past. Their brand of society (often based on over-exploitation of "common people") is extinct. The conditions found in people's lives today have a haunting ring to times past. Super rich elites who lose connection with "common people" ,practice policies focused on short term benefits without concern for long-term sustainable health. Therefore problems like global warming and the opiod crisis's do not draw their immediate concern. How to achieve a better bottom line becomes the concentration of decisions made. These elites run our systems of economics and government and if we are not careful our whole society may find itself in intensive care.

CHAPTER 2

THE ANCIENTS

The ancient world was full of over-exploitation. The Chinese built several projects that by their mere presence reek of over-exploitation. The Great Wall is the best know of these but, the Grand Canal may be even more impressive. According to the "World Heritage Centre" the Grand Canal was first built in 480 BC. Like the Great Wall it started as a series of smaller structures close to each other and then was unified under Emperor Yang of the Sui Dynasty. He wanted canal systems moving grain to his armies guarding against Mongol invasions. Yang was a tyrant who made peasant farmers work on the canal until it was finished in 609 AD. Nobody knows how many peasant lives were spent to create this grand project but, Chinese leaders would benefit greatly for centuries because of the exploitation of these workers.

Tyrants could get unbelievable work done. Alexander The Great, drove his people (mostly his army) to levels they never would have reached without his tyrannical power. His goal of a one world society with Macedonian government and Greek culture made him conqueror the known world. Julius Caesar took an unstable society and brought it back to greatness. His successor Octavian (later Augustus) would set up a system of government and organized economic programs that lasted 500 years. The famous Pax Romana. Then of course there are the Pharaohs of Egypt. No free thinking society would spend so much effort to build a coffin for one person to have an after-life better than anyone else. These achievements marvel us today and hardly anyone can read about or look upon what these often brutal rulers accomplished and not be impressed by the human effort needed to complete such tasks. Yet, there lies the exploitation. What about the workers? The soldiers and peasants who completed these desires of often unstable spoiled despots. We know that Alexander's army rebelled against him and he had to brutally put down challenges to his rule. In fact this is often the way tyrants maintain their exploitation. Brutality combined with cultural loyalty to an often godlike leader is a basic formula for over- exploitation. So the minds of these "common people" were often not set-up for rebellion against the despot, and even if they did revolt, their heart was not often in the rebellion or they simply were easily put down.

So what was the trade off for "common people" to be ruled in a way that over-exploitation was the order of the day. Well we must remember that the exploitation was often inconsistent and spread out over time and effort. Peasant classes often lived out their lives farming , raising families and following the cultural beliefs passed down to them by their ancestors. Many times the over-exploitation was the subtle everyday efforts to feed one's family in circumstances that benefited elites who could rule over vast areas without providing any assistance in making life more reasonable to live. The Czars of Russia knew, the key to ruling Russia was to make sure the peasants "have cabbage in their cabbage soup". This may be one of the most profound statements explaining over-exploitation ever made. Make sure people's lives are just good enough and you can rule over them in ways that are unreasonable in the big picture of things.

The lack of enlightenment in the ancient world can be a strong case for the "common peoples" lack of outcry against over-exploitation. Lower expectations of what life could be and cultural norms (often carefully nurtured by ancient tyrants) created barriers to rebellion. As long as they had "cabbage in their cabbage soup" , they would obey tyrant rule.

This form of over-exploitation occurs all the way to our present day. North Korean leaders have kept their society in a cultural time capsule to exploit a population that still believes in ancient ideals of loyalty to a leader with mythological abilities to control all parts of life on heaven and earth. In the middle east many societies hold to cultural traditions where, by western standards, unreasonable exploitation of people is just part of everyday life. So much a part of their mindset are these exploitative ways of life that many traditional Islamic women cannot imagine life without wearing full bodied burkas or being punished for slight improprieties of cultural beliefs established a thousand years ago in the hard desert environment of the Arabian Peninsula. If people know nothing else, the over-exploitation becomes an easy path for the exploiter to take

Basically the ancient leaders had it a lot easier in over-exploiting their subjects. Enlightenment would take centuries to occur and even when it did tactics of book burning and killing off scholars sealed the deal for rulers to increase their own power and wishes while keeping those "common people' in their place. "Cabbage in their cabbage soup" made life tolerable and allowed the "social contract" (as John Locke put it) to continue. Only when leaders became too lazy or to incompetent to hold these meager requirements was their any attempts at removal or uprising. Oftentimes new exploiters would take over a community and the peasants would learn that they were within the control of someone else. Usually things did not change or if they did it was temporary and the subtle exploitation would soon return.

The reason for this, "same as usual", condition of human life was due to the lack of educated population and the dangers which surrounded most people in their life if a strong controlling presence was not available to create stability. History has proven time and again if the choice is between new freedoms or reasonably guaranteed food and shelter, the masses will take the latter and put up with exploitative practices of whomever can feed them. Such was human life up until the most recent past. Tyrants could exploit and rule over people because they were better than the alternatives of instability, hunger and death. It would not be until these conditions ceased to dominate life that an enlightened age (briefly held by the Greeks and Romans) would soften the need for tyrant rule and give human freedom from over-exploitation breathing room.

Unfortunately the breathing room would be periodically choked off by a variety of well know factors. Different in their scope and intensity due to improvements in industrialization, transportation and communication but, still the same line up that had terrorized the ancient world. Warfare would be top of the list of the old horrors coming back to not only exploit people but, allow tyrannical promises of stability in the face of chaos.

The Napoleonic wars in Europe rose out of the instability of the French Revolution. Napoleon obtained dizzying heights from the failed French attempts to rule themselves and the threats that the rest of Europe put on a society that would dare to take on such a task. Napoleon was able to unite Europe for the first time since Charlemagne and ran France as a military camp. His great fault was he could only function in a state of war. He eventually would lose and leave France in shambles but, came closer than anyone in fulfilling Alexander's wish for a one world government.

Europe after all had spent the previous one hundred years conquering and exploiting societies all around the world. Their form of exploitation through tyranny was called colonialism. With mercantilistic trade (the ultimate in economic exploitation) Europe enriched itself while crushing peoples futures. For Napoleon, it made conquering the world a lot easier. By taking Spain he then controlled over half the Western Hemisphere. If it were not for the twenty two miles of water between him and the British Empire (along with their Navy) he may have had the possible exploitation of the world in his hands. With his defeat, Europe went back to various degrees of exploitative colonialism that would not stop until midway through the twentieth century.

CHAPTER 3

SLAVERY POISONS FREEDOM

The Napoleonic wars lasted some twenty years and cost somewhere around four million lives. Society had not yet perfected the industrialization of war and it's exploitative powers. Society would take a great step in that direction in the next war of that century. The American Civil War. Winston Churchill called it the, "last of of the old romantic wars and the first of the new wars". It was a war run by a tyrannical regime trying to hold onto a system that had matured into one of the worst societies the world has ever seen. The goal slave tyrants had was to take their system of exploitation farther west. A system that brought with it backward development in roads ,schools, and public facilities. Trying to stop this tide of Western slave expansion was the main motivation of Abraham Lincoln and the Republican Party. Slavery took away the promise of America. That if you worked hard and did the right things you could make your life better for yourself and your family while leaving a legacy of a life well spent. Slavery had none of that for Blacks or most whites. Even those who owned slaves lived lives they would often look back on with great regret. Kate Stone, (a wealthy antebellum southern belle from Louisiana and author of the dairy-based-book,"Brokenburn") had the following reflections as a much older non-slave holding southerner," my first recollection is of pity for the Negroes and desire to help them. Even under the best owners, it was a hard, hard life: to toil six days out of seven, week after week, month after month, year after year, as long as life lasted; to be absolutely under the control of someone until the last breath was drawn; to win but the bare necessities of life, no hope of more, no matter how hard the work, how long the toil; and to know that nothing could change your lot. Obedience, revolt, submission, prayers all were in vain. Waking sometimes in the night as I grew older and thinking it all over, I would grow sick with the misery of it all". Fredrick Douglas felt that slavery effected slave owners as badly as it did slaves themselves. The total exploitation of another human being was difficult to square within the soul of many white people. He said of his Baltimore Maryland mistress who had first taught him the alphabet, that keeping him in his place as a slave had the following effect on her behavior,"Under its influence, the tender heart became stone, and the lamb-like disposition gave way to tiger-like fierceness". Yet, this system had ingrained itself so deeply in southern culture that a paternalistic belief by the slave holding class held Blacks as happy in their conditions. Even poor whites bought into this system as one they could not live without and looked to the elite plantation holding politicians to support and enhance this bondage of fellow human beings.

The elites of the South held so tightly to slavery for one very simple reason, they made a lot of money. The South had an estimated GDP in 1860 of three point five billion dollars. That was more than northern society by about one billion dollars. The problem of course was all the money was in land, cotton, and human labor. This cycle (land, cotton, slaves) left very little money for infrastructure. The explanations for these differences developed a calcified political rhetoric combined with violent defense of southern values. In Dr. Joanne Freeman's books on political violence in the Antebellum period, she exposes the willingness to use bowie knives, pistols (and of course in the case of Charles Sumner) canes to enforce the political beliefs of the South. Paralysis of democracy was the outcome created by southern tyrannical demands concerning slavery.

People who traveled South saw the differences almost immediately. No one more than Alexis de Tocqueville, in his observations of the South he wrote,". one perceives that talents and virtues become ever rarer among those who govern" (in the South). Tocqueville observed that elite whites in the south shunned work and had a main goal to,"Smoke like a Turk in the sunshine".

Tocqueville saw that southerners had a more simple life that cared more for keeping a style of life than chasing riches in fortunes and money as he saw up North. Southerners would have loved that reflection. Tocqueville did not study the slave auctions or see that this tranquility was accomplished by the blood and sweat of human property which demanded strict adherence in social and political controls for survival. No deviation from the path of a patriotic southerner. Slavery was good and anyone who wanted it removed was an enemy. No compromise allowed.

Douglas's observations and Kate Stone's regrets all combine to show a compressed path lacking abilities of democratic compromise. To admit slavery was wrong or unsustainable cannot be tolerated in a society based on keeping others down so an elite class can make money.

All sorts of explanations have to come forward in preservation of such a system. Slavery is natural, it is in the bible, and of course the paternalistic belief that slaves were happy in their condition. I am often amused when reading different histories on the reaction of slave holding elites to the outcomes of Lincoln's Emancipation of the slaves. In several of Yale history professor Dr. David Blight's books, it is pointed out that the slaves freed themselves. They left plantations in such large numbers that Northern armies (their main avenue to self emancipation) did not (and often could not) handle all the freedman coming to them. Many southern leaders(including Jefferson Davis, president of the confederacy) were surprised by outcomes of emancipation. Twenty Three year old Kate Stone herself was shocked that all her mamas slaves were leaving her. These southern tyrants had actually drank their own poison on paternalism and how great their society really was. Like Roman masters they had become the victim of their exploitation. The only way slavery's evil could be removed from the United States was by more bloodshed. Lincoln saw this more clearly as his goals would change from stopping the spread of slavery and save the union to destroying slavery and giving the union a new birth free from the tyrannical exploitation that had kept half the country backward and mired in stagnation. Lincoln refused to say war in his early days as president. He would eventually change and call this conflict the Great Civil War. Like all wars it would change only what people could suffer to change. Nobody who lived it would ever forget it.

CHAPTER 4

GREAT WAR

The Civil War happened near the end of the medieval medicine and at the beginning of modern medicine and mechanical abilities. The unacceptable casualties of that war were a result of old time tactics combined with modern technology and medical practices that would horrify people if done on wild animals. For four years two parts of the same country tried to destroy each others will to make war. The North had the tougher job. They had to bring the South back kicking and screaming to a system that would not allow the western expansion of their exploitation of labor. Few northerners were concerned about the exploitation of slaves, they were concerned with economic impacts slavery brought upon areas where it existed. The loss of the promise for a better life was sucked out by slavery institutions. To keep one category of human beings in bondage meant the other categories had to join the slave system and all its limitations. Like the Romans two thousand years before, the lack of individual development became an infectious symptom of slave society. Wealth created by owning slaves was the pyrite of economic improvement. Higher and higher slave owners saw their false wealth increase making them hang onto slavery while banishing from discussions any ideas that might replace it.

Slave tyrants were also very good at explaining their system as the one that held to true Untied States values. It was their society that believed in handshake agreements, self reliance, and an earthy tie to God's teaching. They believed the North had lost it's way from the plans our founders had for society. Industrialization created white people working like slaves in factories, and big city living were all abominations to the founding principles of Jefferson and Washington. Southerners believed the North had entangled itself in legalized federal systems that bound them to a type of slavery where white people were often leveled to same race status. The South was the true beacon of what the founders believed. They sold this message to the poor of the South so effectively that many poor southern whites(people without land, slaves, or future opportunities) bought slavery as a system they could not live without. The un-written contract was that their white skin gave them a get-out-of-jail-free-card and that no matter how hard or bad their lives got at least they did not have black skin. Not all poor whites in the South bought this but, a heck of a lot of them did. So much so that they could keep two large armies in the field for a four year period against an opponent possessing grander capabilities to make war.

Just listen to the rhetoric of these slave holding elites explaining their break from the Union. Alexander H. Stephens (the eventual vice president of the confederacy) said at a Georgia rally in March 1861," the negro is is not equal to the white man; that slavery, subordination to the superior race, is his natural and moral condition. Or there is Robert Tombs (an elite Georgia planter and politician) who went even further and struck at the very heart of what white southerners (rich and poor) should feel was at stake in this conflict. He would say at the Georgia convention,"Republican Rulers, whose avowed purpose is to subject our society, and subject us, not only to the loss of our property but the destruction of ourselves, our wives, and our children and the desolation of our homes, our alters and our firesides" Statements like this and a cultural connection expressed by Toombs to firesides and altars along with family and children, got non-slave holding southerners to feel a bond to a structured system not benefiting their alters, firesides, and definitely not their families. Their slavery support was injected to them more like a snake bite than a drink. Ignorance from poor educational backgrounds and a psychological bond with people who looked like them made poor white southerners sign up by the thousands to defend the sacred land of the South. So they went, marching to an exploited doom which would haunt them even if they survived.

Gettysburg; it's name still holds like Pearl Harbor or 9/11. Probably the most com-memorated (and today) celebrated battle in American History. Dr. Gary Gallager (Professor of U.S. History University of Virginia ,Retired) believes people make too much of the battle. After all the war continued on for two more years. In 1864 the blood letting was beyond human belief. Not until the disasters of WWI would the world see carnage in battles matching the 1864 overland campaign. However, Gettysburg serves the ideal of over-exploitation probably better than any other battle of that war. The reason is that Lee was still trying to fulfill his version of how the war should be fought. In his mind the only way the South could win the war was to bloody the North so badly that they would give in. In Lee's version of victory the South would get the Union Army out in the open and destroy it. To do this with Napoleonic tactics facing modern rifled muskets (not to mention the artillery) would cause mind numbing casualties yet, Lee felt it was the best path to victory. He had used this philosophy at Antietam which resulted in the bloodiest day in American History. Twenty five thousand casualties in a single day of fighting mainly due to Lee's aggressive behavior.

So Lee's strategy is to bloody the North with a Southern Army that had a hair trigger mentality. Many historians feel the southern demand for honor helped develop this tactic. An army of southern boys would not stand for digging in (in fact when Lee had them dig in during the peninsula campaign he received the nickname the "King of Spades"). A definite slap to the command of any southern general. The hair trigger was reflected in how Lee led his army. Lee gave his officers a lot of command room in making battlefield decisions. So much so that ,at times, his generals were not sure what their orders exactly were at any given moment. However, from the beginning it was made clear to all his commanders, timid leaders would be removed. Those who made mistakes being aggressive may face criticism but, would be kept in command and counted on to be aggressive again. By the time of the Gettysburg engagement, his army was undefeated with this strategy. He had repeatedly beaten larger, better equipped, and more professional armies than his own. Lee knew his men were great fighters but, they were not the best soldiers. To fight them was exploiting their strengths and getting away from what he saw was his army and the South's weaknesses. Those being economic staying power, and cultural patience. He saw the enemy in the center and decided to attack where he believed the punishment of a destroyed Union Army could be achieved.

That is the historical reasoning for Lee's attack. It is one I have heard and for awhile took as the gospel for the attack on that line. Yet, there is something missing in that explanation. Something deeply troubling about how a human being given unchecked power over lower ranked people can over-exploit them to the point of annihilation.

If anyone; military expert or not; has been to Gettysburg Pennsylvania and stood in the woods where the confederates started their march and looked over that field of fire, you have to ask, "What the Hell was Lee thinking"? He knew what cannon could do to infantry in open ground. He knew what canister fire (a military tactic of loading a cannon with small iron balls to make it like a huge shotgun) could do to close marching formations. He knew what minnie' balls would do to troops trying to cover large stretches of uneven ground. What was he thinking? Shelby Foote (from Ken Burns documentary on the Civil War Fame) was asked that very question on an in depth C-span program. He said, "Nobody knows what he was thinking and I resent anybody telling me what he was thinking at the time." he further went on to say, "Lee made the greatest mistake of any general in the war by ordering that charge". With all due respect to Mr. Foote and his legacy, if it is such a big mistake shouldn't we try to figure out why? Lee is considered by many to be one of the greatest generals in American History. This guy graduated top of his class at West Point . He had no demerits as a cadet in four years. He was called by Winfield Scott, "The best soldier in the Army". His abilities were proved time and again as absolute genius under fire. Why would a man with those credentials do such a poorly conceived attack. I believe he had fallen into the same trap all successful leaders can tumble into if proper checks on their decisions and behavior are not continually available. He simply over-exploited his army and the men he deemed to be of a lesser station than himself.

All military commanders exploit their troops. It goes with the job. They exploit them in a way that few other professions require. Military commanders must send people into a job and watch them die. Then be ready to send more people into the same job. No other profession requires this type of decision making and it is why we have special schools for them to learn from. The same schools also teach proportionality. Meaning the cost of an act in human life to the objective achieved. Lee lost this understanding. He would get it back and go on the defensive(which he hated) to protect his army and his now more limited manpower. His actions at Gettysburg are so out of line with a soldier of his caliber that to me (again all due respect to Mr. Foote) his thinking was clouded by the willingness to over- exploit those who were under him to a point of their destruction.

This over-exploitation showed directly for Lee. The dismembered bodies all over the wheat field after the battle were proof of his over-exploitation of an army he felt could do his bidding no matter what he ordered of them. Even more profound is the fact that these southerners were (by many people's standards) free thinking citizens. Not people exploited by a tyrant to make huge stone coffins or gigantic canals that benefited only the elite on higher levels. These southern boys attacked for a deeper belief. I have often wondered what went through their minds as they lined up to make the march. William Faulkner stated that all southern boys wish they were in those woods at Gettysburg. When the South was still the Old South. They were over-exploited by their leader. What made them different was these soldiers (each in their own way) were mostly in that charge by choice. Where they misguided? Practically we would have to say yes. Actually for that time and place the over-exploitation was only extreme in the outcome and speed in which it happened. Elites, both North and South, over-exploited "common people". What makes that charge so troubling is what the exploitation was for. The obvious horrors of slavery are hard to feel a sympathy for the loss of people so courageously dying for what they believed in. The evil they were fighting for and how it did not benefit their sacrifice makes a person today feel remorseful for how obviously over-exploited these people were on that fateful blood soaked day.

Not so obvious is the over-exploitation done in many other sections of modern society. Many times it takes years to see the results when a leader suddenly crosses the threshold to exploit people beyond what is reasonable. Like the confederate soldiers who hit the center wall at Gettysburg, these subtly exploited people may not realize how the over-exploitation is hurting their existence. For the confederates the results were immediate. For an over-exploited worker the subtle nature that often happens can be mixed in with confusing information clouding the causes of the results of the exploitation. Things like; less spending power, longer hours, and limited free time can gradually and frustratingly squeeze people's lives. They start to hit a wall of simple existence.

CHAPTER 5

MOM

My mother was born July 15th 1938. I know that date not because I am a great son and gave her a birthday card every year. In fact I am ashamed to admit she rarely got a phone call. I know that date by heart because in the ICU she was dying in the nurses who were trying to save my mother's life had to ask for the date of her birth every time they gave her a pint of blood. She had broken her leg in a fall and had surgery to fix the bone. The doctors had put a steel rod up the side of the bone and bound it together so she would be able to walk within days of the operation. Well, walk with support and therapy. When the surgery was over the assisting surgeon came to my brother and myself and said it had gone very well and that she would be out within the hour. He said she would start therapy by the end of the week and did we have any questions? I cannot remember saying anything to him. I was just relieved to hear my mother would be alright.

Then she came into the hospital room. Something was wrong and several of the nurses could see it right away. My mother grabbed my arm and said , "Get me out of here I am going to die". They had warned us that the anesthesia was making her agitated and be ready for her to have some aggressive behavior but, I believe (even under the influence of that drug) she knew something was wrong. She started to lose consciousness and began to lose eye sight. That's when they put her in the ICU. She never left. For two days they tried to figure out what was wrong and finally found (through an MRI) that during the surgery they had hit an artery in her leg and that she was bleeding to death. We transferred her to a different hospital where they were able to stop the bleeding. However, from the beginning the doctors told us this would most likely be the end of her life. She fought like the tough Irish lady she was for three days to live. Then the last day she fought to die. Pulling the breathing tube (that I had given the ok to put in) straight out of her throat. She came to when I was not there and told the doctor she wanted to live but, believed it was time to die. They told her through dialysis they could keep her alive in a nursing home facility and she looked straight at him and said, "No way, pull the plug." She died some seven hours later. Thus ended the life of what most people would consider a "common person". No statues put up in her memory (although they did put up a flag with her name on it at the senior center). No state funerals, just a simple service with a stand in priest that only knew about her from the things I had told him over the phone. No T.V. Coverage or flags at half mask. Just a "common person" gone.

I will tell you there was not a lot common about my mother. Richard Nixon once said, "his mother was a saint, like everyone sees their mother". Well I can tell you my mother was not a saint and since I was the one who put the tube in her to save her life (when she specifically told me not to) I will not anger her spirit further by calling her one. She attended college at what is now UNI but, was then called Iowa State Teachers College in the late 1950s. Not a common thing for a woman of that time to do. It was there that she met my dad and got a degree in speech pathology. My Parents got married in 1960 and had me in 1961. They would have my brother in 1963. Mom was always the hammer in the house. I of course was the good son. Not because of my innate goodness but, because she scared the heck out of me. She had more trouble with my brother. He was a natural athlete who feared very little when it came to physical activity. He once put a coffee can on his head and had the neighborhood boy try to shoot it off with a bow and arrow. You know, "William Tell" style. The boy shot a little low and stuck the target arrow five inches into my brother's forehead. He then proceeded to walk across the alley and through our yard entering the house proclaiming as he shut the screen door behind him, "Mom, I'm hurt". She turns around from doing dishes to see him standing in the door with an arrow sticking out of his head and blood profusely running down all the canyons of his face. Looking like red rivers flowing down a rock cliff. My dad rushed into the room at the yelling of my mom and grabbed my brother rushing him to the car. They drove him to the emergency room (this is before 911 calls) and I can still see some 51 years later his laying on the table looking around the room with that arrow protruding out of his head. The doctors came rushing in to examine him and after a few quick looks said, "oh", and unceremoniously popped the arrow out of the wound. The smooth tipped arrow had hit his skull and slid up his scalp, burying deep into his hair-line. Two stitches and he was out the door. This was only one of many adventurers my mother would have with her very talented and active son.

Needless to say my brother and I both exploited our mother. As her kids it is part of the job. She once told me she wanted to have ten kids(she was catholic). They could not have had a better mom. Oh, she was hard on us. The main way I got her wrath was because I was and still am naturally lazy. She was anything but lazy and she led by her words, her example, and if necessary her form of discipline. I know spanking is frowned upon today, however, in a German Irish household during the 1960s, to spare the rod meant to spoil the child. My mother had a sorority paddle that had holes drilled in it to get better bat speed to our behinds. She did not do this often but the threat was always there. She instilled in both her sons a work ethic based upon her farther (a hard working Irish salesmen, who started from virtually nothing to make a home for himself and his family). To this day as a retired teacher I get up before dawn looking for something to do. So much for the lazy kid.

In my mother's working life she was exploited beyond what many would consider acceptable. People realized her work ethic and competency very quickly. More often than not this would lead to finding a way to use her so her workplace would improve without compensation for her efforts. She had believed that if she showed her abilities and determination people would naturally reward her with increases in compensation. There was one instance where she reorganized an entire library and it's periodic table only to be laid off when budget cuts came the following year. When she left they asked her for the format she had used in the organization process so they could copy it in the future. She gave it to them with no compensation for her work. At many of the places she worked she often got higher calls for performance without increased compensation. The problem was, she performed like the mouse rolling the ball up the hill, only to have it roll back down again, she just worked harder.

Speech pathology was what she was trained for and where she would spend most of her working life. A Speech pathologists in elder care facilities sees a lot of sorrow. People who have had accidents, diseases and usually strokes. These horrible events often cost them the ability to speak or at least speak clearly. My mother, this "common person", could get prideful people who hated the sound of their new damaged voices to speak again. The improvement in quality of life was substantial. They could now say what they wanted, or more importantly did not want. They could laugh, cry and be understood in ways lost to them before they met my mother. She allowed her patients to exploit her time, her energy, and many times her own mental health in order to get them to improve. Yet, for all of this she never became wealthy. Her administrators often found ways to limit her pay, increase her work loads and enrich themselves rather than compensate this very deserving employee. Speech pathologists did not have union representation or much leverage to increase paid time or benefits. It was not until my mother was in her sixties that there was a major shortage of speech pathologists (go figure) and she was compensated at levels that she probably should have gotten all along. She worked until she was seventy four years old. She told me once she got fifty five dollars an hour at the age of seventy just to sign papers. Of course in typical fashion of my mother she felt really guilty. I said," My God, you deserve it." "Just sign the papers and take the money." She could not do it. She took on patient loads and worked with people up until the day she quit, not retire, quit. Her words.

As I said before my mother will have no statues to her existence. No big parades for her accomplishments. She allowed herself to be exploited by her employers, her patients and her family. She passed a work ethic onto her sons that has been exploited by others many times to excess. No, there will be no monuments, but I will argue there is. My mother's exploited life was once again defined in the ICU room that her sons watched over throughout two dreadful nights. When she was still speaking and could talk to the nurse taking care of her ,she stated, "I loved what I did with my life." "It was absolutely wonderful."

My mother's type of exploited life and the people like her father are what make presidents great and have monuments built to them. Her type of exploitation has won wars and made generals have ticker tape parades. Her type of giving of oneself has allowed countless people to pound their chest and claim greatness beyond their own personal abilities. In fact it is the exploitation of the "common people" of this country that makes America great, not again , not before, but, right now.

This is why over-exploitation by elite people is so poisonous. It is an abusive and vile betrayal of what makes our society potentially the best. Outsourcing jobs to foreign countries , manipulating existing jobs to have low pay, bad benefits and dead end opportunities, making education a secondary concern with college tuition so high only elite people may attend, are all betraying the promise our society claims to have. People like my mother need to be exploited for their talents and work. To over-exploit them is ,in its own way, worse than any of the for mentioned exploitations this book has covered so far.

The egregious exploitation that can be seen is the wealth gap our society shows like a massive puss festering boil on the side of an otherwise healthy animal. How can a person even spend a billion dollars? Do you buy a small country? What would someone need with twenty or forty billion dollars and then why would you demand to have more by the over-exploitation of "Common People"? It is hideous for me to think that four hundred wealthy people own more value than the rest of us combined. What on earth can they have done to earn five million times more than a person like my mother? Do they have some time continuum secret so they work forty hour days? I have no problem with people getting wealthy but, discovering milk chocolate candies or how to connect social media is not worthy of riches greater than the gods.

CHAPTER 6

LISTEN TO THE MUSIC

Johnny Paycheck was born Donald Eugene Lytle in Greenfield Ohio. He later took the performing name Paycheck from a boxer who spelled the name Paychek. He was not well know to people outside the country music scene. He had some hits in the later 1960s and a few in the early 1970s but, it was in 1977 that Johnny Paycheck became a household name. The song was the ultimate crossover hit before people really started thinking of music that way. I remember when I was in High School, you could not turn on a radio for any amount of time and not hear Johnny Paycheck singing his hit song. The chorus lyrics are what most people remember. "Take this Job and Shove It", I ain't working here no more." The song became an unofficial anthem for working people across the country. It's timing resonated with what was going on. I would say the song became a cry (sometimes a howl) for what working people were going through at that time.

In the late 1970s most economists agree that the trend for wages was flattening out while the cost of living continued to climb. The squeeze on the middle class had begun and people were really beginning to feel their lives tighten in a way that had not happened since the depression years. The problem was, there was not a depression. People had jobs, they just could not make ends meet. Oil embargoes had sent gas prices to levels that put substantial amounts of income in a gas tank. The price of certain foods was low (anything with corn syrup or sugar in it) but, healthier choices often carried a high price tag. Land prices and housing increased , which was ok if you owned your home, but, not conducive to obtaining the American Dream for those who rented or were in the market for first time purchases. Cars; that key to our mobile culture went up in price(and if it was a car, or especially a truck that was made during this time it was probably low quality). I remember many trucks would rust out at the wheel wells just a few years after they were purchased. The term rust bucket was used a lot for vehicles that were only a few years old.

All of this was happening at the end of the Vietnam War and Watergate debacles by our politicians. People were fed up with the systems they lived in and you could hear it in the arts of that time. . An anthem, a howl, or a cry for help. For many people the work ethic of my mother kicked in. Literally, women went to work in numbers unprecedented in American History peace time conditions. Giving their families a second income that could help with the rising costs of living. Women had always been workers and now they were heading for careers. No other song (and movie) expressed this phenomena more than "Nine to Five". Which became a number one hit for Dolly Parton.

The exploitation these women faced was higher than the men. Paid less for comparable work, and worked longer in highly productive tasks that brought little compensation or recognition, sexual harassed at all levels with very few avenues for reporting the acts. Most of these overly-exploited women went into the workforce to lesson the financial costs they were facing within their households. Many of their talents were exploited, like my mother, to benefit the systems they worked in. Too often their paychecks had them barley getting by and their intellectual abilities were used with very little credit. There is a section in the song referring to how women go crazy because they love their jobs but, hate the exploitation. How can people love being over-exploited. My reasoning is they love the work and how it gives them an identity but, they hate the over-exploitation higher ups expose them to, and in the 1970s and 1980s those over-exploiters were almost exclusively men. So yes a conflict like that would "drive you crazy if you love it".

Another song that I remember with this theme was Donna Summers "She Works Hard for Her Money" which came out in 1983. This part of the song hits home with a lot of working women(and men) of that time. The song just missed song of the year honors for a female vocalists and again(like the other two examples) you could not turn on a radio for long in 1983 without hearing the song.

So what did this all mean? Does art reflect life? Most historians will agree that it does. Billboard hits may not be the writings of Shakespeare yet, they resonate with people for a reason. The exploitation people felt during this time and all the fallout from it are still with us today. The conditions have had thirty years to incubate and we see the results all around us. The cases of Bill Cosby and Harvey Weinstein show a shift in the reporting of illegal exploitation of people. Imagine the amount of over-exploitation that occurred during these times. People (especially women in the work-force, who needed the extra incomes) were ripe to be over- exploited by those who held power over them. It was during this time (at the height of her career) that my mother was not compensated nearly enough for her work. Like many other women she had to have the job and much of her working life can be found in the lyrics of all three of these songs.

The over-exploitation expressed in these songs stems from the economic philosophies found in free market systems. In these systems people are to follow their self-interests to provide the energy that makes our economy ignite into the powerhouse the world has witnessed for the last one hundred years. My mother and many other "common people" allow their talents to be exploited for compensations that are to create a decent lifestyle. How these energies organize into a free market system need to be understood in witnessing how the over-exploitation is used on "common people".

CHAPTER 7

THE INVISIBLE HAND

Adam Smith was a Scottish economists and philosopher who lived from 1723 to 1790. In 1759 he wrote a book called "The Theory of Moral Sentiments", where he introduced the idea of the "invisible hand". He would later enhance the "invisible hand" with another book in 1776 called "An Inquiry into the Nature and Causes of the Wealth of Nations"(often referred to simply as the "Wealth of Nation"). From these books many leaders enhanced a belief that they often were following anyway, which was to leave society alone and allow the people to fend for themselves. Laissez-faire economics (or translated meaning "let it be") was a product of Smith's beliefs. The concept of the "invisible hand" can become complicated but, basically it is the philosophy that if you let people economically follow their own interests they will then benefit others following their interests and an interwoven free economic system will develop that everyone has the potential to enjoy. Skillful use of resources by "common people" following their own self-interest in a lightly regulated free market will allow maximum resource use and satisfaction for both consumers and producers.

The examples Smith used for this philosophy were the Butcher, the Baker, and the Brewer. In Smith's 1759 economy these business owners follow their own self-interest in maximizing their wealth. To have the best business they must please the customers with good quality items at low prices. By these business people following their own interests the community gets high quality meat, beer and bread at a reasonable price. The Butcher, Brewer, and Baker fulfill their self-interest by developing businesses that create wealth for themselves with the profits from customers coming into their stores. Smith believed that government should only be in this process to enforcement contracts and provide national defense. Any artificial involvement by the government would muck up the works of the "invisible hand" as the self-interest of people would stymie and die on the vine. Taxes should be at a minimum for this free market society to work. People who were in need should be taken care of by private methods and not government programs where the "invisible hand" of self- interest is corrupted. In Smith's beliefs the "invisible hand" was an unseen force for good in society. People were to be trusted to do for themselves what was best and that would then have a domino effect on societal economic structure which unleashed energies people would not normally bring forth. Because people were doing things for themselves they would be more motivated to work harder and more efficiently with a righteous outcome for society.

In Smith's view of exploitation (or what he called fulfilling self-interest) a society will run best when each of us does what is most advantageous for our own existence. To be fair, Smith felt this naturally included people doing what was best for their communities as well. Smith believed that part of the satisfaction of being human was the helping of others and that the Butcher, the Brewer, and the Baker would all take some of their hard earned resources to make society better. This fulfilled their self interest because they would not want to see their community (or anyone in it) suffer to a point of impoverishment. Therefore , programs will naturally develop to help those under privileged souls who for whatever reason cannot keep up with the energy of free markets.

The question is ,can self interest (or exploitation of others) create a natural unseen force to run our society with limited government influence. Will people who have acquired gigantic fortunes through self-interested exploitation of people and institutions give back enough to their community so others are not over-exploited. Or do the great achievers see those who have not created wealth for themselves as lesser people not deserving of their hard earned money and position in life. Recent history tells us there is an imbalance when Smith's philosophies are relied on in modern economic activities.

The economic calendars show 2008 as a year to be remembered. Economists who look at that period, say it was a product of the calendar years which existed before it. Two economists had (with the help of believing politicians) really set the stage for that memorable financial year. One of them would not live to see the year so affected by his beliefs and the other ended up answering for them both. The two men were Milton Freeman and Alan Greenspan.

Milton Freeman was a Noble Prize winning economists who believed whole heartily in the Adam Smith ideal of the "invisible hand" and the exploitation it would develop. He believed that if government agencies were allowed to grow, their own versions of the" invisible hand" would artificially stymie economic growth in the free market. That government officials would follow their own self- interest and want bigger and bigger agencies spending more taxes with limited (if any) benefit at all. This type of self-interest did not enhance people but, made things worse while politicians told society they were getting better. The hammer he could lay upon these programs was the tax money they costs. It was an easy sell. Who wants to pay more taxes? How is it in a person's self-interest to pay more for programs that many people did not see as beneficial to their lives. The salesmanship to see government as evil dropped the gavel as sold in Friedman's auctioning off Adam Smith as the answer to society's problems. Politicians like Ronald Reagan and George W. Bush(who gave Dr. Friedman the "Metal of Freedom") hailed his philosophies as the absolute truth. Very few mentioned the "invisible hand", but, they spouted off its gospel as if brought from the mountain. Friedman believed business owners would do what was best for their clients. Deregulation of business(especially finance) would be the order of the day for the Bush administration. Government spending would be directed toward making corporate America takeoff with incentives packages designed to create an economic no holes barred wild west.

Get big government out of the picture and let big business takeoff and all Americans would benefit. I remember hearing phrases to describe this period like, "A rising tide raises all boats, or "a big meal leaves a lot of crumbs on the table". These phrases say the "invisible hand" loud and clear. All United States citizens would benefit from the activities created by self interested wealthy people. During George H.W. Busch's run for the republican nomination in 1980 against Ronald Reagan, he called these ideas "voodoo economics". A lot of other people called it "trickle down economics" and the more blunt crowd called these policies "tinkle down economics". There were other names I will not use here. No matter what they were called ,they all sung the same chorus, "business is good ,government is bad".

Friedman played this tune and sang the song all the way to his death in 2006. He would not see the collapse of the financial markets which torpedoed the U.S. economic ship and nearly sunk it into the depths of depression. If it had not been for a historically sensitive Federal Reserve chairman and a humbled economic conservative President, 2008 would have been another 1929.

Ben Bernanke and George W. Bush are the heroes of 2008. Bush had the harder road. By developing the TARP program he had to go against every fiber in his "invisible hand", free market, soul. Courage is not the correct word for this realization. He just used common sense. Sometimes the hardest thing to find, especially in Washington. Bernanke used his knowledge of the Great Depression to stop another one. He is a great example of learning from the past. As a former High School history teacher it did my heart well to see someone (besides our military) finally learn from past mistakes. Both Bernanke and Bush threw out the "invisible hand' (at least temporarily) and came in with massive public programs toward finance to boost the economy. President George W. Bush said, " Wall Street had the party and we got the hangover" I have wondered if Bush understood how Friedman's influence had set the stage for the economic mess. Friedman was gone which left the other "invisible hand" believer was left to explain what happened.

Alan Greenspan was the Federal Reserve Chairman from 1987 to 2006. He was a Milton Friedman and Adam Smith believer with a true ability to calm people about complex economic conditions. Using carefully chosen words and actions,Greenspan created confidence in the quasi-governmental agency called the Federal Reserve (or Fed for short). Greenspan seemed flawless in his tweaking of economic indicators while using economic language like a musical composer to calm or ignite investors and business managers. Legend started to develop around this one man in financial circles of our society. He got up early to hear world reports. He stayed late to formulate policy. Wall Street finally had one of their own at the economy's helm. He could hear business reports and know if interest rates should go up or down. He was the man who rode herd over the nation's prosperity in the 1990s. Greenspan seemed to have the code cracked on prosperous times and Bill Clinton let him run the show. The same was true for George W. Bush and the Congress. I remember Greenspan reporting before Congress on the economy(as Fed Chairman often do) and Congress people from both parties were falling all over themselves to gush on this man's reputation as an economic genius.

Then 2008 came. He was no longer the Fed Chairman however, it was obvious his support of deregulation policies had been instrumental in causing the meltdown. Business and financial managers that he trusted to run the economy with Smithian ideals of self-interest and Greenspan's beliefs which supported unchecked exploitation of the economy had blown up in everyone's faces. Greenspan was brought before Congress this time to explain how he supported these activities. His answer is one of the most honest to a failed idealism I have ever heard.

Greenspan simply said, "those of us who have looked to the self-interest of lending institutions to protect shareholders equity (myself especially) are in a state of shocked disbelief." He made further comments on how for forty years he had believed in an ideology which had proved to be incorrect. What is that ideology and why did it go wrong? Greenspan believed in the exploitation of the Adam Smith's "invisible hand". If you leave people alone they will naturally follow a path of self-interest that benefits society. Therefore, everyone can enjoy higher levels of income and quality of life . That the only thing a government should do is enforce legal contracts and provide security to the system. Good government should limit regulation, limit taxes, and make government like that good referee in a big playoff game that nobody notices. That was his ideology. The elites he relied on had their own ideas. They could not help their own human nature to over-exploit the conditions he provided them with and then make their exploitation so confusing and unbelievable that even Greenspan could not figure out what happened. Greenspan learned a hard lesson of exploitation (one that Milton Friedman never learned) people are too greedy to leave without barriers. Especially when you are talking about trillions of available dollars. How on earth could he expect financial institutions to monitor themselves. The evidence was clear before 2008 that wealth corrupted people would over-exploit the system to gain billions in value that benefited no one but themselves.

Greenspan should have known that a multi trillion dollar economy with billions of transactions everyday cannot be run on a philosophical foundation with it's basis being a Butcher a Baker and a Brewer. What was he thinking? I believe he fell into the same trap as Lee at Gettysburg. Greenspan like Lee is a brilliant , and I believe honest man, who simply allowed "common people" to be over- exploited. He believed that a deregulated economy would work for everyone. He believed in the brilliance of U.S. financial institutions. He believed the economy (that had made him look like a genius as the Federal Reserve Chairman) was invincible and would not let him down. He believed that business would have the interest of "common people" in their actions either intentionally or by the mythological functions of the "invisible hand". He believed that Wall Street would be the defender of Main Street and that these elite bankers with their rise in wealth would float all boats to a higher level. In other words he actually thought these financial graduates from Ivy League schools of business cared ,or at least, by their activities, would do well for Joe and Jane from Main Street U.S.A. In the end this brilliant man looked like a fool.

What Greenspan and Friedman did not understand from their ivy league towers was you need to balance out the exploitation so it exists without over-exploiting people. Like that referee in the big playoff game, there needs to be someone to call a foul, someone to call strike three, and someone, if need be, to change the way the game is being played. Having very competitive people who's main self-interest is to make money, call their own balls and strikes is really a ludicrous idea. Imagine a Bears Packer game (or insert your favorite rivals) with no officiating. Nobody would pay to see the game. As frustrated as people can get with officials (myself included) we must have them to regulate the competition. The same is true for government financial regulation. Yeah it slows down the game, Yes it limits profits however, it does not let us get out of hand. These regulations prevent exploited people from becoming over-exploited. These economic downturns do not exploit the wealthy. They can easily weather the storm. The 2008 economic downturn hit the "common people' the hardest and in many cases they have yet to recover from the over-exploitation.

The formula many corporations and financial institutions use is based on over-exploitation which can have a wide net for the people they over-exploit. Deregulating this formula intensifies it's effect on "common people".The formula can have several different types of ingredients with the same ending results. The highest sought after result is to make a lot of money for already very wealthy people. This formula uses the "invisible hand". However, instead of the Adam Smith "invisible hand" that will do good through self-interest of the individual, this use of Smithian ideals is based on one way exploitation that quickly matures into over-exploitation of "common people".

What is the formula? As previously stated it can take on several forms. The most common one for financial institutions is to find something in the society that is creating value. In 2008 it was housing. Home values were rising at 20% a year. That kind of increase spreads blood sent in the water to financial sharks who can't help themselves in trying to get in on such increases. These sharks began to develop investments which were based on the home values and their increases. They based their investments on mortgages of American "common people",who are widely known to pay their debts. They then overvalued these mortgages (leveraged them) to create future value, that really wasn't there yet. Again this is all based on the idea that "common people" would pay their bills. Nothing really wrong with this formula so far except that these creators of wealth saw their formula was in trouble. Home prices were starting to stagnate. They had based the selling of these investments on prices going up in the future and homeowners being able to payoff their homes. This wasn't happening anymore. Greenspan understood the right thing to do was to invest people's money elsewhere. Instead many investors saw an opportunity to fulfill their self-interest and get wealthy off of others misery. They created a confusing trail of investing, which on the surface looked profitable but, in reality set their own investment clients (and the rest of the country) up for failure. Then they purposely bet against the same investments. They created enough confusing information that it would be highly unlikely they would be prosecuted for wrong doing and made more money than gods as the rest of the country sank beneath the waves of economic recession. If you missed the formula here it is., find value, exploit the value (no matter who it hurts). Then create confusing information about how you did this so you cannot be held accountable. The same formula is used in manufacturing only it is based on actual physical products. The key to the formula is the confusion. If they do not create enough of it companies can get caught. When you see executives having to explain why their products had a flaw and where put forth anyway it is them trying to deal with this formula gone wrong. Planes that crash , tires that blowout, emission standards not followed, and children or other illegal workers making products , are all examples of this same formula. Find wealth and exploit it. If you can do it morally and legally great. If something underhanded needs to be done. Make sure it is confusing and hidden enough that "common people" will not figure it out. Again, even Greenspan was not sure what had happened or how these financiers had duped the system.

The results of this type of institutional exploitation is often confusion of where the exploitation has come from and what has happened to the exploited. The mixture of cultural beliefs in individual responsibility and freedom to choose, help in the confusion of the exploited and benefit the exploiters in pointing away from their actions. If something goes wrong, work harder. People should be responsible for your own decisions. Nobody forced people to go into debt, it is their own responsibility. That is the American way. These where the beliefs of my mother. They are beliefs which have made our country what it is today. When this individual responsibility ethic is over-exploited, the fabric of society starts to tear and the beliefs of hard work begin to dissolve into pools of sorrowful anger. Even then the exploiters of this work ethic can point away from their activities toward other parts of society. Often these exploiting entities can explain away how their energies in following self interest damage the abilities of "common people". When large numbers of the population cannot pay their bills , lose their jobs, lose their homes and see their retirement dreams disappear , they are often left with a mixture of shame and anger that can be easily used to win elections while enriching elites even further.

Why are these "common people" over-exploited. Are they just lower creatures who cannot understand and therefore deserve to be treated this way? My mom (introduced earlier as a "common person",) gave me a good lesson in why this happens. She asked during a Christmas Holiday about John F. Kennedy. Since I taught history she wanted to know what I knew about him. She had seen a documentary on JFK's life and had questions about his time as president. I started to tell her what I knew and then about half way through an explanation I said, "wait a minute, you were in your twenties when he was president." "Did you not pay attention to what was going on?" Her curiosity soon turned to a darker mood and she gave me that look that only a mom like mine can give and said," I had two little boys to take care of and a job to work at, my nose was to the grindstone and I did not have the time to know everything going on around me." I am sorry to say she walked away and did not ask anymore questions. A real bonehead move on my part. However, I learned a very important lesson as a historian. When your nose is to the grindstone, you cannot be the greatly informed citizen our democracy often requires. My mom was no dummy. However, her situation in life did not allow for deep intellectual thought on JFK or any other official. She would not have had time to understand financial formulas purposely confusing to hide over-exploitation of her life and that of her sons.

The bulk of society does not have the time or the knowledge to understand how these forces(as seen by the economic meltdown in 2008) can have such a devastating effect on their ability to follow their own self-interests in their lives. The "common people" often lash out at simplistic reasoning as to how failure has occurred. Illegal alien conspiracies, unpatriotic beliefs by evil Americans, even religious explanations of not being Godly enough.

These explanations (as crazy as they often times become) are easier to point blame and understand verses the main reasons for the squeeze. The complex international connections of outsourcing jobs, the huge profits acquired by retail giants buying low price products from manufacturers using child labor, subprime mortgages and the investing practices from them (that were so complex lawyers in Congress could not figure them out), and the continual replacement of labor with robotics, are all damaging working Americans. The exploitation is the result of wealthy people following their own self-interest. Just like Adam Smith and Milton Friedman believed, people will follow economic forces that give them the greatest satisfaction in enhancing their own wealth. As these practices hurt the "common people", elites financially support political campaigns that will deflect responsibility from their actions. Think tanks and political PACS work tirelessly to develop arguments and strategies that will get these hurting people on their side while using the self-interest of the "invisible hand" to pick their pockets.

How else can a reasonable person explain the rise and political win of a self-serving egomaniac like Donald Trump? Only a scared and confused electorate could believe that this billionaire would have their best interests in mind. An electorate that had been influenced to go against their own self-interests. An electorate fearing the changes around them and how they no longer felt the "America's Promise". That promise being that, my life will be better than the life of my parents and I will leave a legacy of a life that will be better for my kids. To accomplish this feat I need to work hard and be self-reliant. If I accomplish that I can work my way up the ladder of success and enjoy all the benefits of that journey. My own home, two car garage, two week vacations, and of course an eventual comfortable retirement . Again hard work is the key to this dream. Hard workers makes our country great. Like my mother, people who love their jobs and allow a major portion of their lives to be exploited so they can get the return exploitation of a job well done and a life well lived. A life with comforts acquired from this hard work. A life filled with possessions and satisfaction that make the hard (and not always enjoyable work) worth the exploitation. When this promise is no longer there for a large majority of the working class people in our society an explanation needs to come forth. This is the "cabbage in the cabbage soup". The question is, are today's "common people" comparatively getting more than the peasants of Russia?

CHAPTER 8

THE RESULTS OF OVER EXPLOITATION

What will be the results of over-exploitation to "common people' in the United States (or anywhere for that matter)? Well, take a long hard look at two categories of over-exploited people in our society today. These over exploited peoples warn all others about complexities created when depriving generations the development deserved as legitimate citizens. African Americans and Native Americans are two of the most down trodden categories of people in society. Both have made great progress from their earliest horrors in over-exploitation yet, they both statistically show the deep unhealed wounds created like a dull machete chopping it's way through their history's. They were forced down different paths of over-exploitation however, the effects are very similar. Both have low economic development. Both lack proper representation in our society. Neither are excepted in our country as full participants in many areas. Both are blamed as the victim. Meaning their poor condition in today's world is somehow their fault and they need to forget the past and pull themselves up by their own efforts. As the saying goes, Pull yourself up by your boot straps. One Native American chief told a reporter who said that to him. "Moccasins do not have boot straps." In other words, Don't start using your cultural values to explain our situation.

Even with the profits from casinos. Native American Reservations are still one of the worst places in the North American continent to live. There are higher levels of alcoholism, obesity, and high school dropouts than any other single place in the United States. Unemployment is high and suicide can run in cycles that are found among no other people. All a person has to do is read a history book to see the over-exploitation this population faced and it is a wonder to think any of them are alive today. Multiple attempts (at different times in history) to wipe them off the face of the earth. The use of tactics (that in any age would be considered barbaric) were freely practiced against these proud people. Diseased blankets traded into their villages (usually with small pox) helped spread epidemics that killed thousands of Native Americans. Total warfare practices against economic resources (killing off the Buffalo) while mounting purposeful attacks to kill women and children in their homes were given the blessings of United States society as we moved our self proclaimed superiority to the West. Yet, we expect these same people to pull themselves up. Taking all their land , destroying their culture and trying to simultaneously train their youth to be good white people while using policies which would extinguish future remnants that these great peoples ever existed. Over-exploitation of this severity found in anyone's background kills off future development. Native Americans for many decades could not imagine a future with the expectations their exploiters enjoyed as they used Native American resources and exploited the benefits gotten from the continents original inhabitants.

The proof is in the statistics. From the U.S. Census in 2012 on Native American life, damage by over-exploitation is blatantly apparent. Native Americans have the lowest employment rate of any racial category. Native American students score lower on standardized test and graduate from High School in numbers lower than any other students in the continental United States. Probably the most telling of these statistics is from an EPA study in 2012 that showed 120,000 Native American homes lacked access to basic (again basic) water sanitation. So much for the wealth from casinos.

Many would argue that Native Americans have a lot of perks provided for them by society to get them out of these conditions. There are programs (such as free education) which many believe should break the cycle of poverty and repair historical damages brought to Native American society, are not enough. Damage to the essence of a people's being may never be totally healed. How do you heal spirituality, especially if it was based on physical earth centered conditions which no longer exist. Ripped away from the Native American was what made them unique and valuable in the world. Uniqueness (that if exploited properly) could very well have solved many of our problems we face today in 2020 Imagine learning how to take care of the earth from a people so closely tied to it. Instead of destroying their ties to the land, we could have learned exploitation that would sustain into the future in a better way than we have done or are doing today. We would not need a sixteen year old from Sweden to alarm us that things are bad. Native Americans could have made us more courageous in our development and not over-exploit what we found when we took this continent. I do not want to sound too Polly Anna here. Europeans taking over the western lands for future exploitation was inevitable. The over-exploitation of the people that lived there and the resources we found was not. That history is on us. So is the needed patience to help these proud people back to the greatness they once had as one of the most earth-centered people who ever existed.

African American history and over-exploitation go hand in hand. When I taught American History one of my goals was to have our students see how the over-exploit-ation African Americans faced in slavery and in the times of Jim Crow created the over-exploited damages we see in society today. Yet, nothing can show the damage better then the actual statistics. According to the U.S. Census statistics, African Americans experience poverty at 21% compared to whites who experience poverty at 8%. The Census also reports that the average white household had an income 30,000 dollars more than the average African American household. Who was the only category of people who experience more poverty and lower incomes?, you guessed it, Native Americans. This gap has narrowed recently and the good news is that many African Americans are staying above the poverty line. Again according to the Census, this achievement is very much due to government programs. Free school lunch and SNAP (Supplemental Nutrition Assistance Programs) have helped many people (not just African Americans) keep their families fed with good foods.

Still the damage is all around us. Achievement gaps for African American students have been a problem for years. Many of my republican friends have stated that other minority categories have found excellence in education, why not African American students? Is there something wrong with them? Asian Americans often succeed very well in our education system. In 2018 the average score on the ACT for an Asian American (according to the College Board release on the Admissions Insider Web Page) was an average composite of 24.5. In the same group of statistics was the African American ACT composite score of 16.9. This is alarming since most col-leges(until recently) will not accept ACT scores that low. When my republican friends look at this difference their perspective is that it is because African Americans do not try as hard. My friend's "invisible hand" philosophies and white person's ex-periences (or what many would call the white privilege) goes quickly to the idea that these people just don't work hard enough. To have government programs fill this gap is a waste of their tax money. Get them (African Americans) to work harder. Strive for the American dream, follow your self-interests and the "invisible hand" of the market place will take care of itself.

Although historical time and situation differences make comparisons a somewhat dangerous endeavor, I cannot help but see the same lack of vision over-exploiters in history have had to the exploited. Why can't my Republican friends see the damage. Many of them are over-exploited white people who work their tales off just to make ends meet. They listen to modern versions of Johny Paycheck songs and complain often about the modern squeeze on their lives and the limitations they face. Yet, they look at a category of people who have received none of their benefits as white people and believe they should somehow being doing better. It is a paradox W.E.B. Dubbois saw often in his trips to the South. White "common people" and Black "common people" were more alike in the problems they faced as over-exploitation formed their lives. Cultural divisions due to skin color was an artificial separation of peoples living parallel existences. True, white people had a get-out-of-jail-free card with their skin color but, there were not many other perks in society for them during W.E.B. Dubois observations. What kept these two over-exploited populations from banding together is similar to the reason the confederate boys charged the wall at Gettysburg. If whites "common people" were to rally with African Americans ,then they would be at their status level. That status level carries a stigma in society hard, if not impossible ,to over-come. The stigma is an ugly vein of poison on the cultural body politic of these United States. We can try to cover it up with social niceties and appropriate outrage at public leakage of the poison by politicians, police , and others in power. However, this venomous self-inflicted condition will destroy us if we allow it to continue. In the end the artificial separation allows for over-exploitation. Although it does not happen often, whenever Black and White vote together in our democratic system, change does occur. The abilities of elites to over-exploit is diluted to the point of shifting self-interest to working with the "common folk" in order to maximize their outcomes. This potential antidote would have to become a routine outcome of the democratic process to shift exploitation practices yet, it could happen. Indeed it has happened.

CHAPTER 9

THE SPEECH

Barrack Hussein Obama was born in Hawaii on August 4th, 1961. Some people, Donald Trump for example, tried to have him born in Kenya. This would not have mattered anyway because his mother was an American citizen which would have made Barrack an American citizen anyway. For those looking to create scandals against this "common person" the details did not really matter. Barrack would grow up in a world that recognized him as an African American. In his first run for president he was portrayed by some as not being black enough. He would respond by saying he was black enough not to be able to hail a cab in New York City. The response was typical of this product from a white mother and an African father. Both university professors. The father was absent from his life while his mother's side of the family helped raise this very talented (and often a little lazy) young man. He would gain worldly experience. Africa , Malaysia, and brief stays in other parts of the world would open his eyes to how life was for many people on this earth. His intellectual abilities would eventually lead to Harvard and legal training that had him thinking of being a judge. When he was told he needed to be more relaxed and personable in debates with Mitt Romney in the 2012 campaign he would remind people that at heart he was a constitutional judge, not some kind of comedian. Although he could do comedy from a script. His timing was very good, however, if he went off script he often failed to get laughs and remarkably acquired a Johnny Carson-like ability to make people laugh about not getting a laugh. A lot of this had to do with his "common person" roots. He seemed to never forget them. Nowhere was this more evident than the speech he gave as a Senator running for the presidency in 2008.

The place was Philadelphia at the National Constitutional Center. The date was March 18th 2008. Barrack Obama's presidential campaign was in crisis. Reverend Jeremiah Wright had given a series of speeches from his pulpit at the Trinity United Church of Christ in Chicago that spoke very negatively of the United States society and it's treatment of African Americans. The Trinity Church was where Barrack Obama and his family attend services and the Reverend Wright was the pastor he identified with. Barrack Obama's opponents had seized upon the speech's to show him as identifying with the hate the Reverend Wright portrayed about U.S. society. Most campaigns would see this as damage control. In fact many people in his campaign were exactly in that mode and wondered if the Obama campaign could survive this challenge. Barrack saw the situation as an opportunity. He had danced around the race question up to this point and now he saw an opportunity to take it head on. He told his campaign managers he knew what he wanted to say and on March 18th before a live audience and national T.V. coverage he gave one of the most amazing speeches in American History. The official name of the speech is "A More Perfect Union", many of his campaign workers referred to it as just "The Speech". It hit a nerve in the United States of 2008 and every time I read it that nerve is still triggered over a decade later.

Barrack Obama used the speech to explain the anger of Reverend Wright and where it came from. He then went on to say that the anger was real and part of Reverend Wright's generation but, was not realizing the changes our society had accomplished by 2008. He further expressed where he thought our nation was at in 2008 and in doing so expressed what only a person from both social worlds could explain to the rest of us. He exposed the reality of many Black people and the overexploitation they experienced. The inability to live a good life. The shame associated with unpaid bills and frustrated conditions of wealth inequality were the traction to a better future for themselves and their kids slipped into the fractures of racism both hidden and exposed. He revealed how institutional programs had limited African Americans from obtaining the American Dream creating categorical states of depressed achievement which on the surface my republican friends identify as self-inflicted laziness. He gave his community belief that (unlike the Reverend Wright who saw these conditions as unchanging) there laid ahead of African Americans hope for a better and more involved future. One where as Martin Luther King said, "they would be judged not by the color of their skin but, by the content of their character". Barrack could have stopped there and had a very good speech . However, he went further and made it (in my opinion) one for the ages.

In the spirit of W.E.B. Dubois , he stated how White working and middle class Americans were experiencing their own form of over-exploitation. Disappearing pensions, outsourcing of jobs, and down waging of incomes had all created frustration in the White community. This made them feel no particular privileges because of their skin color and fostered resentment toward any suggestions their place in life was earned in ways unavailable to others. White populations felt rugged individualism combined with hard work was why they lived in better neighborhoods with higher performing schools and less crime. The over-exploitation of their category confused and angered them at the same time. Someone was to blame. The macroeconomic forces working against them and over-exploiting their core values of hard work and individual responsibility created a lashing out that was seen in the Tea Party movement after 2008 and the eventual election of Donald Trump in 2016. They are still lashing out. The most recent example is seen in trying to support an ever increasing unsupportable presidency that promised to make their "America Great Again".

For me Barrack Obama's speech helped explain my republican friends (who I am still tied to and probably will be for life). They are hard working tough minded people who would (and in my case have) quickly give their shirts off their backs to help someone. Many of them were hurt by the 2008 meltdown and many of them lashed out blaming the welfare state and over taxation of new programs like Obamacare. They voted down referendums to fund their schools and projects for new streets, parks, and libraries. Their formula for dealing with over-exploitation was to pull into themselves as much as they could and rely on the things they took pride in. However, their pride was not always enough to get by. Several of them had to take unemployment benefits. They had to insure their families with universal child healthcare. School lunch programs that offered free and reduced meals helped feed their families. Yet, they held to the ideals of self-reliance and would continue to resent all attempts to point out the hypocrisy. The prideful ideals of being white and self-sufficient are often harder to penetrate than the African American street toughness created by years of dealing with over-exploitation. Many times both groups will pridefully stay divided without seeing how mutually beneficial combining forces could be. W.E.B. Dubois noticed this in the early 20th century and Barrack Obama noticed the same problems in 2008.

The whites have the advantage in staying divided. During prosperous times, when more than "cabbage is in the cabbage soup" is available, they acquire enough means to economically segregate themselves from the Black community. This helps solidify the separation. Nobody need divide and conqueror a force that is already divided. The elites of society benefit from this the most. In 2016 the electorate was so divided that a president bound to help no one but himself and the wealthy people around him, won and spread our social crevasse even wider. The over-exploitation opportunities become endless. One way or another this crevasse cannot sustain itself. The short term gains to elites by it's existence and the over-exploitation possibilities they have will soon cave into one of two scenarios. Number one will be the complete deterioration of our society. Number two will be a coming together by "common people" of all races and creeds to form "A More Perfect Union". There really is no third option. In Barrack Obama's speech he tried to point this situation out to all of us as only a person who lived directly with both conflicts could possibly articulate. Seeing our society laid out in his words brought hope for the second option(A More Perfect Union). President Obama once said that in observing his kids and the interactions with their friends that,"They are better than we were ". I have witnessed this as well among my students. I tell them at the end of our sections on reconstruction and the "Jim Crow South" to make their kids better than they are and maybe someday we can suck the poison of racism out of the nations veins and cross the crevasse that artificially divides people who have more in common than they know.

The problems with this divide is it allows over-exploitation to occur for both working and middle class whites along with African Americans in the same economic situations. Rationally it makes no sense for either human situation to somehow think the other one is against them. Barrack Obama tried to point this out in his speech. For those of us straining to explain why our society was separated along these lines he hit the nail on the head. The speech did not solve the problems, nor was the Obama presidency's eight years in office able to bridge the divide. Yet, we saw, even for a moment in time, what can happen when enough people come together from these two camps. Not only the election of the first African American president but, also passing into law legislation that had been tried and failed for over a century. Obamacare is of course the landmark accomplishment of President Obama's time in office. To our present day Obamacare's achievements are the gold standard for accomplishments against over-exploitation of "common people".

CHAPTER 10

HEALTHCARE

Universal healthcare is something our society has tried to have since Teddy Roosevelt. Over one hundred years of failure due to the idea that healthcare is the same as being able to afford a better car or live in a bigger fancier house. Beliefs (usually by people who have high incomes) that healthcare needs to be earned through a person's occupation or increased wealth. If a poor person gets cancer, those are the breaks. That individuals should have found a way to afford higher coverage in case of a catastrophic illness. The Adam Smith ideal of an "invisible hand" driving the market will have people follow their self-interest to obtain better healthcare. These ideals can only come from someone outside the "common people" arena of life. Unless you have a situation where you are one hundred percent sure cancer is in your near future, you do not plan to get it. There are too many costs and needs in the immediate present for someone in the working class (or even upper middle class) to set aside the massive amount of resources needed to handle cancer treatment expenses. It is absolute hogwash to believe the "invisible hand" of the marketplace will handle this problem. High expense healthcare should be like the roadwork our society has to support people and their lives. Roads free us(rich and poor) to move through society and improve our existences on earth. We build these roads together with successful outcomes to business, family, and cultural enhancement. Think how we would function if only the wealthy could use a road effectively. Our communities would lurch along at greatly diminished levels we might think as normal if forward thinking leaders in the nineteenth century had not decided to make them a public expense. How able might our society be today if those politicians in the Teddy Roosevelt administration made universal healthcare an American standard? Instead of people and businesses scrambling constantly to afford insurance premiums and medical costs, we might enjoy the same smoothness of life that publicly funded roads now give us. After all, government programs are what are society does when it wants to accomplish something together. This is not an evil process. We have educated millions of young people in public schools. Taken care of those same millions when they are older through social security. Fought and won wars against tyranny. All with publicly funded programs.

Orin Hatch (Conservative Republican from Utah) and Teddy Kennedy (Liberal Democrat from Massachusetts) reached across the ideological differences they both had to pass universal child healthcare which has saved thousands of families from financial collapse while attempting to treat their children's unforeseen health challenges. Free market energy would not accomplish the humanitarian outcomes of child healthcare. Hundreds of young lives become futures with hope under a public program devised by political rivals who saw the needs of "common people" and turned down a road to help.

These are things an advanced civilized society should do. I know of very few people who would look at a child's sickness and determine the "invisible hand" of the marketplace should take care of them. Like when a weakened beast in the jungle is devoured so the strong survive is the ideals of over-exploitation in human society. To deny socialized healthcare with "invisible hand" ideals cannot be found in any other higher technical society in the world except the United States. This is obvious over-exploitation. Working at jobs that do not provide decent benefits or do not pay enough to individually buy good health insurance is a product of years in over-exploiting "common people' and the society they live in. We should be able to see that a person with crisis medical conditions needs systematic help that combined resources can provide.

Yet, in 2016 many "common people" voted against universal healthcare and for a candidate and a party looking to destroy the very system that would help them. Similarities to yo-men confederates charging the wall at Gettysburg with irrational logic toward their own interests and their very existence. In 2016 a mixture of fractured "common people" reacting to our first Black President who wished to use his presidency to benefit people in need clashed with counter strokes lashing at government and huddling back to individualized responsibility and free market remedies. Free markets cannot deal with complex social inequalities where profits interests rarely reveal themselves as the solutions. As that southern yo-man in the 1860s, these working class people saw answers in a system that had eight short years before brought them to the edge of economic ruin. Massive government intervention was necessary to avoid collapses of epic proportions. People bought a formula for success handed to them by a New York billionaire who's harsh banter of elites and promises for renewed old-time prosperity made white voters hurry to his banner. His confusing descriptions of Obamacare were helped by poor implementation of the program. Saying statements in crude basic terms made Trump's message resonate with angry "common people" who lack the time or the knowledge to look into the details of what Trump's message on anything was (especially healthcare). He succeeded in igniting a loyal base who would charge the walls for him and his mixture of ranting rhetoric and confusing facts. Trump said , "The polls, they say I have the most loyal people. Did you ever see that? Where I could stand in the middle of Fifth Avenue and shoot somebody and I wouldn't lose any voters, okay? It's like incredible,"

Is this not the same type of loyalty those confederate soldiers had when they hit the stone wall? Promise them cabbage in their cabbage soup and they will allow you to lead. He has not killed Obamacare yet, If he wins again in 2020 I cannot see the system surviving. The "common people" would once again hit the wall for the elites in our society with limited benefit for themselves.

CHAPTER 11

EDUCATION AND ROADS

I was a teacher for thirty three years. My first seven years were not very well done. Some people are naturals in a classroom. I was not. I struggled with the fear of not controlling a class so the educational process can take place. Very few people understand the delicacy the learning process has within it's functions. Distractions in learning can take place by people simply walking by the door or window. Students talking out of turn or entering the classroom with alternative motives to learning can make the environment untenable for education. My early career was spent focusing efforts on control so students could learn. The learning often fell second to the control due to the fact I was not skilled at dealing with disruption cleanly so learning could recover quickly. The only remedy I found to this challenge was to be highly organized and create a structured classroom environment that smoothly ran from one educational tactic to another. How to have structure and freedom to learn combined into my lessons took me an entire career.

Teachers (even bad ones as I was) will tell you that how you teach depends on the students you have in front of you. Classes full of talented students are a breeze to teach. Students who are not motivated to learn can give even top teachers challenges. The key as I saw it, was to have a class structure which could effectively teach motivated and non-motivated students efficiently in an environment where both teacher and student got along. This is the other factor of education that is hard to explain but, crucial to success. The relationships between teacher and student can make all the difference in the success or failure of learning. To achieve this balancing act with young people takes a talented well trained individual or (in my case) a lot of trial and failure with hours of work formatting a well planned structured environment which promotes learning. Once this environment is achieved, continual and constant maintenance is required to keep it. Teaching becomes a twenty four hour endeavor. You hardly ever leave it completely. There is always something to improve on. Even in the summer break you will often find excellent teachers at their schools figuring out ways to perfect their craft. None of this extra time is paid for and the overall pay for many teachers is far below the average payed to most professional people. The talents of a great teacher need to be exploited by their students, the parents, and the community. Great teaching can help students achieve beyond their natural abilities and change life goals and paths more than any other profession. Like my mother I truly believe I did good work with my life's career. I am proud of the accomplishments many of the students who worked in my classrooms achieved. Yet, teaching by it's very nature can be set-up for over-exploitation more than most professions. The over-exploitation of the teaching profession will lead society's future downward and out of leadership contention in solving the world's problems.

We already see this in so many areas of science, math and literature. Our international educational rankings are middle of the road and have not moved in years. Many politicians talk with two mouths in funding public education. On camera mouth number one praises the promise of good educational opportunities ,while in back rooms mouth number two states how do we cut the budget and get money away from those greedy teacher unions. My own state of Wisconsin is the perfect example of this say- one-thing-do-another mentality.

Before the economic crisis in 2008, Wisconsin was considered one of the best states in the union for public education. Then a formula was developed by elites looking to take control of Wisconsin's government. Step one of the formula was to create divisions between private and public sector workers (especially teachers) that makes private sector, workers hurt by the Great Recession, support cuts in public sector contracts so tax breaks can be given across the state. The formula was an easy sell. Hurting people who had lost their jobs and benefits due to the crazy investment adventures by bankers following deregulation lashed out at identified unrelated causes. Trying to explain how the Great Recession happened was difficult to do. Saying teacher contracts were too high was easy. After all almost everyone has gone to school, and almost everyone has had a bad teacher. That person who just wasn't into teaching or had burnt out in the profession. Having that image portrayed as normal gave the hurting workers of Wisconsin an enemy to lash out at. Freeloading, benefit rich, and overpaid teachers were sucking the lifeblood from the hardworking taxpayers in the state. In their fear and confusion the "common people" of Wisconsin bought this nonsense and elected to the governorship an "invisible hand", confusion formula believer named Scott Walker. Walker would create legislation known as ACT 10 and Wisconsin is still trying to recover from it's effects.

Act Ten took away the rights of teachers to collectively bargain for their wages and benefit packages with their local school boards. According to governor Walker it gave local school districts the tools to cut their own budgets as he cut the state funding to schools by over one billion dollars. He then painted public workers(again especially teachers) as the reason for much of the economic troubles in Wisconsin. The selling points were that teachers had been living high off the hard working cash strapped taxpayer. Huge salaries and overgenerous benefit packages were bankrupting Wisconsin. He used his brother as an example of the average Wisconsinite. He tended bar to help pay for insurance benefits that would cover him and his family plus his regular day job. Walker's message was that teachers needed to work as hard for their money as other Wisconsinites. That for too long teachers had been coddled by the state. Republican lawmakers gave interviews calling these budget cuts" little nicks" compared to what "common people" in Wisconsin were suffering. Overall the formula was extremely successful. Walker survived massive protests against Act Ten and a recall vote. He was caught on video before he implemented Act Ten telling a wealthy Wisconsin donor his strategy in dealing with the teachers was to, "divide and conquer." His formula would have devastating effects for the state's education system but, the confusion created to hide Act Ten's legacy has yet to be unraveled. Nine years after it's implementation the 2019 school year shows the beginnings of Act Ten's over- exploitation.

Before governor Walker, teachers in Wisconsin were already under attack. A republican governor named Tommy Thompson had enacted a spending freeze on Wisconsin teacher contracts called the QEO (Qualified Economic Offer). This program was not directed at any other public worker contract. The QEO singled out teachers to freeze their salaries (including benefits) at 3.8 percent increases. Now a 3.8% increase on salary is a nice bonus for almost any "common person" however, this included insurance. The school boards negotiating the contracts could go above 3.8 percent but, that was not often done. In fact at my school district for six full years no pay increase was made on salary. The QEO resulted in a six year pay freeze yet, we kept the benefit packages intact.

The reason benefit packages are so important to teachers is because it is still a profession dominated by women. Most women were the second income in their families. To have good benefits was important to their kids and so they often traded benefits for salary (especially when they are young). The other reason is historical. In the 1960s and 1970s (when medical insurance was not so highly priced) school boards would offer benefits instead of salary increases and limit their budget expenses. This process was very effective. Again the female dominated profession would follow it's self-interest and agree to better dental insurance or vision insurance instead of a pay increase. As a result when I got my first contract to teach in 1986, my salary was a whopping 13,900 dollars. Many of my friends who graduated from college with similar degrees were making twice that amount. The trade for benefits instead of salary had lowered compensation to the point that talented individuals(especially women with more opportunities in a modern workforce) looked elsewhere for careers.

To be the only income on a starting teachers salary required a minimized lifestyle . Small apartments, used vehicles, and hamburger helper were the regular parts of a young teachers existence. Being in the flower of youth, health benefits seemed like something not all that important. As a young teacher you half listened to the old dogs in teaching lounges saying how important those benefits were and why we would be glad to have them as age weathered away the granite of youth. Now as one of the old dogs I have a greater appreciation to what those veteran teachers told me. However, they never told me the state I was in would elect a governor who would make it possible to take away those hard earned benefits. The years of sacrificing wages for benefits led to a formula for over-exploitation which is ruining the education system in Wisconsin as we speak. If not reversed the students in our state will be the big losers. Motivated young teachers do not need huge contracts. However, they do need to feel a career choice as a teacher will not be frowned upon as some kind of greedy blood sucker that takes from the community. As a teacher going through Act Ten (and many teachers across the country seeing similar programs put against them) that is exactly how many of us felt. We were a brotherhood and sisterhood of over-exploitation.

I did not always feel this way. My early career was concerned on the craft of teaching. I was bad at it. I wanted to get better. The only way I could figure out how to improve was through long hours at school planning my lessons. The habit took and never left throughout my career. The danger of working so hard at something is to be over-exploited in a way many people see as self inflicted. To me this response has a hypocrisy with it that frustrates the process toward excellence. Unless a person is tremendously gifted, extra effort is necessary to achieve higher outcomes. In many occupations the extra efforts are not highly rewarded. The result for many workers is to avoid over-exploitation by only doing what is necessary. In teaching, these workplace survival strategies had the effect of limiting commitment, developing poor instruction, and damaging the learning process of the students. The result is a killing off of the great equalizer that education promises to be. Even the best students cannot completely overcome poor instruction. Throughout my career I did not want to be the teacher who burned out from the over-exploitation I felt around me. When I felt it coming I quit. Many teachers do not. Either due to finances or out of spite they stay in the classroom and poorly train students for their futures. I do not blame them as much as I do a system that pays false praise to the importance of education and then will not compensate the single most important element in the education process. Good teachers. Teachers that are highly motivated and believe in what they are doing. To over-exploit these people is the greatest betrayal power elites can bring to our society. It is also the easiest to pull off. Take the formula used in Wisconsin by Scott Walker.

As I said earlier, Walker gave local districts like mine the tools to balance their budgets by taking away collective bargaining. He then cut over one billion dollars from the education budget. Gave small tax cuts to the hurting working class, and then used the proceeds to entice business opportunities in Wisconsin. He then proceeded to redirect small amounts of increases in his years as governor to education in areas away from teacher salaries. He continually said statements like , "we want more bang for our buck," or the classic, "we want the money to go to the classroom". Both of these gave the message that teachers were not the important part of education. The important thing was where the money was going. He actually was trying to starve teacher unions. Don't pay teachers they can't pay union dues. Meanwhile he skillfully expressed to the public that he wanted better education for the students in Wisconsin. He and his insiders knew these policies would have a negative effect on quality of education. He needed to hide any results that would show the downward turn. The answer was in the testing.

The ACT test had been the standard test for college bound students to take in Wisconsin. The test was taken at their expense and would often give them an idea of their college eligibility. The important point was that in Wisconsin (as in many states) only students planning to go to a four year college took the test. Wisconsin often ranked first second or third in the nation. Before Act Ten I cannot remember a lower ranking than third. Walker realized his cuts would lower this score and Wisconsin's ranking and he could envision the headlines. "Act Ten Causes Wisconsin to Drop in ACT". To avoid this the formula of confusion was applied. Walker had all students in Wisconsin take the ACT at the state's expense. He relied on the ACT to determine how Wisconsin schools were doing from here on. The results were predictable. Wisconsin dropped in ranking and the explanation was easy. Everyone is taking the test, and in schools like mine where not all students were prepared for a four year college level examination they brought overall scores down. The change slipped past the "common people" in our state like a ship in the fog. People without the knowledge or time to look into what Act Ten did to education barely noticed how schools and the classroom environments changed. How teacher moral dropped creating workplace stagnation. The vigor many teachers had gone into classrooms with started to leak energy like an inefficient engine chugging along unnoticed except to the most expert mechanic.

Walker's formula did more to education than to the classroom. New teaching candidates were harder to find. In a recovering economy where teaching should be a profession showing more increase the effects of Act Ten were devastating. In the little school I taught at we had a science opening. The position was posted in all the available outlets, even the local paper. We had two responses with applications. Only one of them was qualified. Another example of this decimation was in 2012. our school had a science intern who was doing her last semester of teacher training. I got to know her a little bit as she passed through the hallways. One day I asked how her job hunting was going. I remember how stressful finding my first job was for me and was ready to give verbal support to help with how stressful the process was, instead she told me that it was going very well. She had sent out sixty application to jobs and got sixty responses. This impressed me because I had sent out nearly one hundred applications when I first came out of college and did not get anywhere near one hundred percent responses. She told me that many of the schools wanted her to just show up and teach because they had nobody else. She further said that in the college of education at her university that she was the only science teacher in training at the college. That her college usually had one hundred and fifty teachers in training and that now they only have thirty eight in all different areas of study. When I told my republican friends about this dire situation they all told me I should thank Walker for his policies. In their perspective he had given my profession "invisible hand" qualities of scarcity that made it valuable. As an educator my mind went to the alarming question of who did the other fifty nine schools get for a science teacher? How were those other fifty nine schools going to teach science to future doctors, engineers, botanists, or veterinarian? Maybe at one of those schools was the untrained student who would cure disease or develop technology to benefit us all. These were the results of Act Ten in teacher recruitment. Walker's policies had all but eliminated a generation of teaching candidates. The results of this may not be felt for years to come. This of course adds to the problems for "common people" to understand. Walker is safely out of office and can blame whatever shortcomings in education on those who come after him. When will the damage be repaired in Wisconsin (or all the other states with Act Ten type programs) so that a science opening will have qualified teachers filling them again? The hard to answer questions are part of the formula of confusion. The formula worked for education but, it failed Walker when it came to roads.

Walker tried to use a similar formula with roads that he had used for education. He pulled money away from the road funds. Redistributed it to business opportunities and tried to explain his reasoning that road funding should be more localized. He had two major problems in doing this. Number one (like education) Wisconsin is known for having good roads. This goes back to a biking tradition (both motorized and manual) that has made Wisconsin a destination for Harley riders and peddle bike enthusiasts. Go across the border into a state like Iowa there is a lot of gravel on back roads causing motorcyclists and peddle bikers to gravitate toward the pavement found on Wisconsin roadways. The problem with this tradition is upkeep. Wisconsin roads need continual repair. The winters freeze and thaw the roads so spring time is pothole time in Wisconsin. Repairs literally cost billions over time. Some of this cost is paid by the federal government and some by local entities. However, a large chunk has to come from the state. This is a burden. Gasoline in Wisconsin is higher than in surrounding states due to a gas tax used to maintain the roads. Tollways which are used in states like Illinois did not fit the Wisconsin image of open visually pleasing travel. How to cut the budget to roads and keep the roads at levels Wisconsin wanted was a problem he could not talk himself out of. He could not create a confusing formula of explanations with the roads, why? It deals with problem number two.

Unlike education (where the results of student learning may not be realized for years) the deterioration of roads in Wisconsin happened quickly. Grumblings about poor roadways hit the media before Walker got to his second term. By the time he had decided to run for a third term the complaints were over whelming. Road construction companies bonded together with a campaign to build Wisconsin roads back to normal. They had advertisements throughout the state against Walker's policies. Even my staunch republican friends complained about how bad the roads were in many of the areas they drove in. Walker would find he had gone to far. He lost his bid for a third term in office. The loss scared the republicans in the legislature so thoroughly that funding for roads was one of the first areas they addressed after the election. The advertisements by the coalition of road construction companies were less frequent as spending on roads increased. All across Wisconsin new road construction could be seen by the miles of orange barrels everywhere. Walker had been defeated. Not because he diminished educational opportunities for kids. He was defeated because he could not come up with sufficiently confusing information to explain away a pothole.

You cannot see the potholes in a first graders education. You cannot see that she does not read at the level she should. You cannot see that budget cuts that were made when she was six years old have lowered her options when she is eighteen. People can see a pothole. "Invisible hand" believing over-exploiters in think tanks around the nation took the lesson that you can trash schools and get away with it but, keep the roads paved or you are out of power. The new "cabbage in the cabbage soup" for Walker was the roads. What he has done to the education system in Wisconsin will create a rough ride for many years to come.

CHAPTER 12

THE ELITES

Needless to say, these writings have been hard on the wealthy elite people in our society. Now it may seem counter to those writings to have a chapter of the book dedicated to them. Religious writings rarely devote a chapter to the devil. She or he is always in the narrative but, hardly singled out for recognition. That would be glorifying the evils presence.

The reason to devote a part of the book to wealthy people is because I believe they are crucial to our society's health. Unlike Lucifer they are not inherently evil. Many wealthy people are hard working, talented, caring and responsible citizens of our country. In fact several of them are ,and have been the best we have. Sam Walton was the ideal American businessman, Steve Jobs was the ultimate in innovation, and Bill Gates and his wife have shown themselves to be the most incredible philanthropic people our society has produced. All of these people used great talent and energy to develop business enterprises that were the envy of the world. Our society needs their abilities to thrive. Yet, they cannot engage in the over-exploitation of the "Common people" for that to happen. Like a shark eating it's own tail to satisfy hunger pains, the wealthy will destroy , not enhance society. Over-exploited people do not work hard. They do not try to achieve at higher levels. As I said earlier , in education this is a catastrophe, in business it means the losses of the very things these people try to achieve. Too many people in this elite category have fallen into the trap of Robert E.

Lee. They are undefeated and they push their self-interests at the over-exploited expense of people in their hire and society as a whole pays for it. Sam Walton was a man who tried to balance out this very difficult condition. To do what Walton did you have to exploit your workers. Yet, for most of this highly energized businessman's life he did not specifically try to over-exploit people.

Sam Walton ironically contemplated in his own book as to whether his life had been well spent. He had cancer and knew his time was limited. He even said his friends would probably be surprised to hear he was thinking this way. I think he was just showing he was human. The retail empire he built is second to none. It is not perfect by any stretch of the imagination. Shortly after his death revelations of buying products from child sweat shops in Bangladesh were revealed along with part-time hiring practices that stopped "common people" from earning a living wage. However, the legacy of the Arkansas Ben Franklin store owner seemed hard to tarnish. He outworked almost everyone in his organization. He learned to fly so he could scout out new store locations and fly to stores in his expanding empire and meet people in person. If he saw sloppiness at one of the locations heads rolled quickly and he replaced the poor worker with workers who had energy. He gave video conferences to his stores trying to rally his workers. His corny ways came right out of the back country of Arkansas yet, it worked. People felt like they belonged to something special.

The specialty did not just stop at feeling good. In the early days workers got to share in Walton's wealth by buying stocks in his stores. Some of these workers became millionaires as employees of Sam Walton's empire. He exploited them however, he allowed them to exploit him back. Walton would travel hundreds of miles to visit stores and find out how they were doing. I worked for bosses who would not travel one hundred feet down the hall to see how I was doing. Walton had stores do cheers and morning meetings to get workers fired up for their day of work. He stated in his book that the hardest thing was to get that kid stocking the back self of his store convinced that their job was important. To many it may have seemed corny and a waste of time to do the cheers, travel to stores, and constantly send the message that your job is important yet again, it worked. Sam Walton's stores became the place for people to go and get the best deal for their money. Then something changed.

As I said before, shortly after his death a lot of disturbing information came out about Walton's business. Yes he had built an empire. Yes he had made billions at a time when to be a billionaire was still a very rare thing. Yet, it seemed toward the end Walton's drive may have done to him what had happened to Lee at Gettysburg. He had won so often and had demanded so much of himself that instead of just exploiting the talents of the people under his empire he may have over-exploited them to fulfill what drove this brilliant American Entrepreneur. In his memoir he stated that he treated the competition he had with other retailers like he was in a state football game against an opponent. He used the same mentality and motivations that had made him a star varsity football player in high school. In fact all of his sons went on to be football players and I believe all of them were on State Champion football teams just like their Dad. No small feat. The same drive which gave his High School a state championship also may have dangerously sent him into the rabbit hole of over-exploitation. Push the limits, even if those limits meant outsourcing supplies to countries with very questionable labor laws. Cutting full time jobs so people working at his stores did not receive full time benefits. Then worst of all creating confusing information on how all of this was working to "Buy American Whenever We Can" campaigns. American flags flew freely in commercials with charging semi-trucks labeled with store logos and patriotic songs. Racks of clothing showing eagles and red white and blue colors giving the impression that everything was American made. In reality that shirt a customer bought for nine dollars and thirty six cents on a roll back price was made in a far off land by workers not old enough to drive a car and paid next to nothing for their efforts. How could this happen? If Sam Walton was still on the hook in the decision making of his retail empire why did these hurtful policies take place? What was Sam Walton thinking if he allowed this chapter to be written in a true American success story? Again I go back to Lee. Brilliant people in charge of those deemed lesser than themselves without true checks on their decisions simply over-exploit from the positions of dominance that they hold. Like the old football player that he was , he apparently saw an opening and called the play to win. The play had an illegal formation but, there was nobody there to make the call.

Talented motivated people driven to a profit motive like Sam Walton cannot be left to their own devices on what they do and cannot do. They will find a way to defeat their competition. Their methods are often legitimate and based on outworking or out thinking their competition. The problem is human nature. When that opportunity comes that can make their efforts payoff ten fold if only they skate the system a little bit and can explain away their actions while relying on the ignorance of "common people".. They will do it. Make no mistake. The power of success and wealth obtainment is just too great to overcome. The "invisible hand" becomes a stab in the back for those people effected by elites and their actions. We see it all the time in the news. A car company cheating on emission standards, A drug company raising the price a hundred fold on life saving devices, An established banking firm creating fake accounts to enrich themselves, and the list goes on. All of this is over-exploitation.

So how do we stop the natural tendencies to have the over-exploited masses charge the wall. How do we keep a system fair and exploit the talents and energies of a Sam Walton? Since our "invisible hand" system is based on competition, we need a referee. Like any good referees or umpires the official needs to have a neutral view of the game. What team is playing or who wins or who loses is not their concern.

That neutral system is what helps keep us free. Rich or poor , powerful or weak, no person is to be over-exploited by anyone else. The same system protects our power elites as well. So the next Sam Walton can climb the ladder to success but, not pull it up behind him so no one else can make the climb. This system is of course our ,and I mean every-bodies government.

To make sure the game is fairly executed is the government's reason for existing. Our society is set up for our government to be like a good umpire. A system that is suppose to work with and if necessary be above the elite economic forces in our society. The government needs to be a useful tool keeping society free and productive without the over-exploitation of those who have profited from the free economic opportunities free markets provide. Unlike a sports game. Our social activities are the serious consequences of lives lived. Not everyone can achieve billionaire status. Bad luck, unequal talent, and differences in motivations create inequities that no free society will ever get rid of. I knew millionaire status would not be my outcome as a career teacher. So my motivations were elsewhere. Still there should not be systematic punishment for that type of motivation otherwise their will be no teachers if we follow the ideals of the "invisible hand" and self-interest only toward higher wealth. The system we have should see over-exploitation as a penalty and remove whatever is creating that situation. The problem (as I have related with Wisconsin's example) is the very systems we freely elect to protect from over-exploitation are often caught in the web of powerful interests. These economic elites often see their place in society as above those who fail the millionaire motivation test. A person who chooses paths not toward wealth is an inferior either by talent or by choice and deserves over-exploitation as their lot in life. Since I am a "common person", I hang around a lot of people with the same motivations. Most of these people I have know are the best you'll ever meet. Our society needs to exploit the talents and work ethics of these imperfect perfected people who's love of family, freedom, and their communities make us all strong. Like my mother many of them go to their deaths thinking life was wonderful. Knowing these people makes me even more angry that they become faceless parts of society to those who hold the reins of power. That by their actions these powerful people over-exploit to a point where the visited memories at life's end would be of an undignified life. These people are tough and like my mother can take a lot. Yet, like everything there can be a breaking point and the millionaires and billionaires of our society know that point is being pushed to limits our society cannot afford to go. So why do they keep pushing the over-exploitation? Why see how far they can go and risk losing it all ? Like the slave owners in the South the answer is simple. They are making huge amounts of money. Some of them are richer than the gods. The desire to increase this wealth (like the slave owners of the old South) blinds them to what they know is better. We seem to be short of Abraham Lincoln's in our modern world. Waiting for one to show up may be too late. This is why we need the elites to shake off the wealth goggles and see what is happening. They have the power to change the system more than anyone.

I do not know many millionaires, and I certainly know nobody personally who is a billionaire. From all the problems I see them get into, it appears to me that wealth does not make people more superior than anybody else. They do have the opportunity to develop a false superiority. Time and again our system has shown how people of wealth generate unequal and therefore exploitative influences on the United States government system. Government officials will help spread the confusion formulas to gain support from wealthy donors to their campaigns for re-election. This is like paying the umpire before the game. The unfair influences acquired allow the over-exploitation that strains our society. The confusion formulas powerful people can use to hide their tracks often create unforeseen consequences as "common people" attempt to navigate these falsely created conditions put in front of them. Free thinking people getting confusing messages to why their lives and families are being squeezed to points where hard work and dedication no longer matter often find undesirable solutions or expressions to deal with their plight. Divide and conqueror is a key to the over-exploitation. If over-exploited people, White, Black and Brown came together to peacefully vote then these wealth corrupted officials would be voted out of office. Our system would be more accommodating to the "common people" overnight. If elites join in on this system , nothing will stop our society from being that "More Perfect Union" we strive for. In 2008 I believe we saw the glimmer of what can happen. For all his abilities , Barrack Obama could not get the elites on his side. Indeed it was his one great failure. In future elections a candidate, republican or democrat, that can join those forces legitimately and serve them as a true leader will really make our country the place it potentially has always been. Truly great.

CHAPTER 13

THE CONFLICT WITH ADAM SMITH

Why do wealthy elite people over exploit others at such a high level? Why can't they all be like the early Sam Walton entrepreneurship. The answer is in the way free markets operate and to understand them we have to see the frictions between a true free market and the ability to obtain reasonable (and sometimes huge) profits as a business. First we need to know what a true free market under Adam Smith's "invisible hand" must have to operate in a way that would maximize the self-interests of people like the Butcher, the Baker, and the Brewer.

For a free market to function the way Adam Smith wanted six basic conditions must occur.

Number one is that there are no barriers to entry in the market. If another butcher wants to start a business in town there cannot be laws or regulations which make a new butcher business illegal or difficult to set up. There also cannot be a meat producer so huge that our Adam Smith Butcher has no chance of competing. Open entry means anyone can start up a new business and compete with the others. In this part of his theory there could be thousands of competing businesses for the same product in any large market. Number two and three are that there can be no seller or buyer big enough to set prices. In short no monopoly type business models who can lower or raise prices due to domination of the market. Number four is there can be no trade secrets. Someone cannot have a better way to make pork chops. That information has to be shared. In this way everyone has the opportunity to make the pork chops with the same ingredients and quality. This leads to item five which is perfect and truthful information provided to everyone to the point where it is perfectly understood. Either everyone knows about an upcoming event that will influence business decisions or nobody does. The reasons for this condition makes sense if the market is to be free. Number six is that the government is involved to enforce contracts and provide security to the system. Government is not to make business easier for one entity over another. The example would be if in a baseball game the umpire came from behind the plate and helped bunt the ball. Government should be limited and neutral.

Doctorates in economics are not necessary to see problems with this recipe if applied to a large complex system. Just take item five as an example. How will their be perfect and truthful information to everyone and on top of that make it perfectly understood. Complexity provides for confusion. Sure the economy of Adam Smith could come close to these requirements but, a modern trillion dollar economy struggles achieving even the basics of Smith's theory. On top of the complexity of our system is the self-interest of businesses to achieve their maximum profit. To attempt this goal using Adam Smith's theory is next to impossible. The only division between a profitable business and one that goes bankrupt would be who works harder and can provide the highest quality product at the lowest price. Think of pharmaceutical companies running by this method. Where the only way they made money on their drugs was to make a better one at a cheaper price than anybody else. Once they made a miracle drug everyone else would be able to make it because the new information that made the drug possible would have to be available to everyone. Only a brief time to have a corner on the market for their discovered drug. Not the decade long copyright laws they enjoy today. So if big complex companies do not run by the Adam Smith "invisible hand" format, what do they use to make their huge profits?

In 1979 a Harvard professor by the name of Micheal E. Porter came up with his own theory on how business actually runs itself to make a reasonable (sometimes gigantic) profit off of it's efforts. Business's had been doing many of these practices for along time, Porter just identified them. He came up with five forces necessary for business to succeed and since his book on this subject they have often been referred to as the Porter Forces. The Porter Forces are as follows. Number one is an established business wants high barriers to entry. In other words you do not want a lot of other people to enter the market with you. If an airplane production company has a series of accidents in one of it's models , a major protection for its survival is that not everyone can start up making airplanes and put them out of business. The complexity of setting up manufacturing centers for airplane production insulates an existing company from failure. Other barriers to entry could be artificially created by the government. A powerful business could lobby government to pass laws making competition for their product very hard to create. Many times government contracts for defense will follow this pattern and shut other companies out of the bidding. Number two relates to number one. No substitutes for your product or service. People who run oil production can get sloppy with their activities because there are not a lot of substitutes for oil. Pipelines can leak, oil platforms can have accidents and super tankers can run aground because people cannot run their cars on pea soup. However, peanut butter manufacturers better be on the ball. There are a lot of substitutes for peanut butter. Some of your best business people come from products with a lot of substitutes. Number three is do not let a lot of information out to your competitors and/or your labor. Keep information from them. You do not want your workers to know how much you made. In negotiations with labor over salaries the key is to hide profits from workers so they do not know your profits as much as possible. Along with labor you do not want your competitors to know any developments you have that are making higher profits. Keep the ideas in house. Number four is to control your buyers. Be the one place they buy your product or service from. You do not want the buyer to have a lot of other choices. In other words be the winner of the monopoly game as much as you can get away with. Number five is to know the strategies and actions of your competitors. So while you are keeping secrets from them, you cannot allow a competitor to have secrets from you. According to Porter's theories these are basically what a business must try to accomplish to achieve a profit in a free market. I confess to taking away a lot of the economic professor speak from his definitions but, these are basically the five ways business can profit by the Porter Forces.

Notice anything? They are almost the opposite of the "invisible hand". The friction between these two theories could not be more obvious yet, they play out in our economic systems everyday. Politicians will spout the Smithian ideals barking against government control hampering the rugged freedom of the United States economic system. While that charade is happening, board rooms of major businesses are trying to limit competition, hide information from their customers and their workers, and manipulated government activity so nobody else can easily get into their area of business. During 2008 they called this too big to fail. The massive size of investment banks made the government come in and bail them out or the whole economy would implode. This is the reason George W. Bush (expounder his whole political career of the goodness of free markets) had to bail out the economy with government money.

The purified cloak of Adam Smith's free market is thrown into the spin cycle with the reality of towels containing the Porter Forces. These soiled garments hold within them secret economic deals, exclusionary tax breaks, and confusing information to keep labor and consumers properly in their places. By the time the wash comes out what is suppose to be clean free market practices has all sorts of added stains making "common people' scratch their heads wondering what in the world is going on. These are the basic ingredients of the confusion formula. So wacky and out of control can this formula get if unregulated we get what happened in 2008.

Why do you think Donald Trump does not want to release his tax records? They are probably full of Porter Force type activity that even with a total release of documents it will be difficult to unravel how the Trump business empire ran itself. The problems he has faced in running the government with backdoor deals and secretive wrongdoing is Trump the businessman following the Porter Forces. When he is caught he tries to make the information so confusing and loud that people feel like they are in a spin cycle. How they come out of it usually is determined by the ideology they had going in. In other words, they fall back on what they know best without reasoning what may have actually happened. This is why he can claim to be able to shoot someone on Fifth Avenue and not lose a vote. The explanations are so crazy he can win when he loses.

I am not saying every business person has read Micheal Porter's books. In fact Donald Trump probably has not. In my own experiences people who have economic power over others just naturally fall into these practices and that is what Porter identified. To make money in a true Free Market is hell on earth. People will gravitate to other methods and that is where Porter's theories come into play. Doing this does not make them evil it just makes them human. They need rules for the game or they will continue to gravitate to wider and wider distances from a free market. You do not have to be a big player for this to happen. In my own little economic environment I have seen the Porter force's used in two different ways. The first way I was directly involved in while the second way I pretty much just witnessed it happening.

I became the chief negotiator for our teachers Union in 2006. The reason was that under the Wisconsin Qualified Economic Offer program toward teacher compensation (as I mentioned earlier) our staff had not received a raise in salary for six years. In my case this was really hard to swallow. I was my only income. We had kept our benefit packages but, that was not buying groceries or putting gas in my car. There were enough people in the same boat as I was and a small movement started to figure out how to get a raise. In the negotiating process (we could negotiate in 2006) I became very frustrated with our financial administrator and school lawyer. Neither of them could tell me how much money the school had in it's budget. They kept saying the numbers were a moving target and it was like a checking account where you could have a lot of money in it at one time and not much at another time. I stated that even a checking account has to have an idea of how much is there to use for expenses or a person will be in financial trouble. They then stated it was not exactly like a checking account the school budget was more fluid. They further went on to say how too much money for teachers would possible damage facilities and equipment buying to enhance education for the kids. See the Porter forces at work? Do not let labor know how much you have available. Keep that number a secret and make the whole situation as confusing as possible. I doubt either of those two people ever read Michael Porter's books. They just automatically fell into those patterns. Grudgingly the school did give us a modest raise and magically they had plenty of money to buy items and manage facilities for the upcoming school year.

The second example was with a business in our local community and their relation to the school. Every school in conducting it's activities will need to obtain services from businesses. Banquets , homecoming parades, and repairs to facilities all require dealing with businesses to keep the school year going. In one particular area our school had found a good business deal that provided us with what we needed at a reasonable price. The problem was the business providing the service was outside the school district. One of the businesses in our district that could provide this service went to our school board and demanded that from now on our school should deal with them and them alone since they were within the district and a taxpayer to the school. The demand worked .For the remainder of my time in that district every activity requiring the service provided by that business went through them first. They had applied the Porter Forces of limiting competition for their service. Again I doubt anyone in that business had ever read Michael Porter's ideas. The drive to follow self-interest led to limiting the competition. Limiting the competition they faced did not make them evil or criminal, it just made them normal. So normal that I do not remember anyone at the time arguing with the business owners about their proposal. Yet, if we were to follow the true ideal of Adam Smith we would not allow the barriers to entry that limited the competition. If Adam Smith's theory is not allowed in a small environment like our school district imagine how its theories are muddied in the wider economy.

The friction between Adam Smith's "invisible hand" and the more realistic Porter Forces are part of the confusion people feel in dealing with our economy. The Porter Forces are not illegal to do in our society unless you were to take them to extremes (like killing off your competition Mafia style). The forces just naturally happen. To enhance the friction between these two economic forces is the enormous size many companies achieve. The larger a company is the more resounding their use of the Porter Forces will be. A large retailer can drive their competition out of business with a supply line that controls sellers and eventually the buyers in the market. Some companies can employ so many people in this country that if they show signs of going under the government must bail them out or risk economic collapse. All of this goes against the "invisible hand" free market ideals of Adam Smith. Why then do we believe it? Listen to the verbiage. independent, hard working Americans. Private sector business makes America great. Rugged individualism and the American dream. It all goes back to those early days when this country was first created. The image of that frontier farmer working his (many times her) fields feeding the family while improving their station in life for themselves and their children. Thus developing the true American citizen that will develop a deep sense of patriotism and personal pride. As this individual rises in the world our nation rose with them to heights greater then the Greeks and Romans ever achieved. All of this is accomplished independently free from invasive government programs, rules, and regulations. The Porter Forces don't fit that image but, the "invisible hand" does. It sounds so good. In practical nature of things some of the "invisible hand" is definitely there. I have seen it. I taught it to my students for decades. I still believe in self-reliance being the best way to run a person's life. Yet, to believe the fairy tale that free market is based on self-interest is the way our society works is ridiculous, foolish, and child-like. Politicians will often sound this way when supporting private business(especially those which donate to their campaigns). My republican friends will push that the free market is totally free and to talk of it as anything else is unpatriotic. Yet, they will want good roads, complain about the schools and want help when the private sector lets them down. This is the mixture between reality and what actually takes place that we all live in. In this reality lies the seeds to over-exploitation. For if you believe one thing and are actually doing another your reality becomes all messed up. If the hard work of "common people" does not lead them to successful outcomes but, instead to over-exploitation by systematic forces looking to rig the game in their favor, then our modern lives are sadder than those of ancient people over-exploited by despots. The ancient people knew their lot in life. Our modern lives become a struggle to reach a mirage that is not really there.

CHAPTER 14

THE EARTH

Scientists tell us we have definitely over-exploited our planet. So much so that in the not-to-distant future we may not be able to live on it. There are still those who want the over-exploitation to continue.

This is a maddening situation which has led to protests around the world. The most recent by a sixteen year old Swedish citizen named Greta Thunberg. Her impassioned speech at the United Nations told world leaders how this unusually aware sixteen year old saw her future and the future of children yet unborn. She questioned why world leaders would talk about profits and stabilization in the present when on the horizon there is a cloud obviously bringing a storm of destruction to the earth that would come to fruition in her lifetime. In her voice was the confusion of a person who clearly understands what is happening when people in leadership positions follow the status quo and allow disastrous outcomes to happen. I can imagine the same passions in the voices of people like Fredrick Douglas fighting slavery or Susan B. Anthony fighting for the rights of women. You do not have to imagine the passion when hearing speeches by Martin Luther King for Civil Rights or the students from Parkland High school fighting for more reasonable gun laws. We can hear the question in their voices. Why does no one care? What all these impassioned people are fighting is the over-exploitation which allows people in power to make huge gains at the expense of the safety, futures, and even lives of other people.

In the case of climate change the science is clear. Either we limit carbon emissions or our future on this planet as a species cannot sustain itself in our present conditions. We will not be able to live, eat, work, or improve on this earth as we have enjoyed for the past five thousand years. Life will continue. Our earth is a really tough place. However, human existence will be in question with massive die offs of people in the most vulnerable situations. This is our future. How can a person in a powerful situation with the ability to exploit their power for the betterment of future generations(including their own future families both born and unborn) make decisions which do exactly the opposite of what is right. We do not need to look too far into the past to see this same situation play out in our own history. Slavery and it's defenders show the same human conditions as those who resist changing our present situations in fuel consumption and lifestyles as those old antebellum politicians defending self- gratifying over-exploitation that benefited the few while the many suffered in their wake.

Slave owners could see that their society was behind the non-slave systems in the North. They simply chose to ignore facts held directly in front of their faces. How could they possibly do this. The easy explanation is the most correct one. As I said before, they were making a lot of money. Today's leaders cannot imagine what would happen if they tried to change the fossil fuel industry or the beef industry. How much money and revenue would be lost. Like the leadership of the antebellum South, they will happily go along toward a diminished future as long as the present and immediate future is not disrupted. The free market will handle our problems over time and if climate change becomes profitable to prevent, the free market will respond with new business models expressing the change.

These answers carry a huge gamble with odds against the "common person". What will happen as we wait for the "invisible hand" and it's magic touch. Will Florida be under water? Will hurricanes hit the gulf coast so often that people cannot live there? Will populations in fringe areas of human habitation be wiped from the face of the earth? Many of these questions will be answered after these leaders (and myself) are safely dead.

In the answers to climate change lay the complexities of over-exploitation. I am a perfect example of this complexity problem. I am not wealthy or elite in power. Yet, I leave a carbon foot print that can and should be criticized. I burn wood to heat my home in the winter time. I drive a car (and until recently) drove it to school each day by myself when carpooling would have limited my carbon emission. I eat beef. Mostly processed meat that is cheap to buy. I have tried to reason this lifestyle much the same as elites reason their decision making. I cannot afford an electric car. To heat my old farmhouse of a home with solar panels or wind power would cost thousands of dollars I do not have. I felt it was important to get to my workplace early and often leave later than anyone else wanted. I often watched people who carpooled crunched for time because the carpool was waiting for them as they dealt with last minute problems. I could stay late and as a result of driving myself finish work and handle problems at my leisure. All of this meant that I was part of the problem more than I should have been. Was the trade off worth it? Could I have been a better steward of the planet? The answer is of course yes. However, before I beat myself up too much for being an emissions hog and killing off future generations of the unborn. I need to make a defense that is not just an excuse.

I (like so many other "common people") am a product of what the society's powerful people have set-up as a place to live in. Like the yo-men farmers in antebellum slavery, I have lived under the conditions presented in front of me. To get to work I needed a car that burned fossil fuels. Like slavery, the yoke of fossil fuel dependency happened gradually over time. If a person looks at the development of the world since fossil fuels, the growth is absolutely amazing. In the time and place of fossil fuel use, the United States became the dominant world power. So as a "common person" within this system I just flowed along. Swimming up the stream to go against what was happening seemed a foreign idea. I would hear of people living in the woods, free from electricity and plumbing and it would seem a very strange way to exist. In fact the area I live in has a large Amish population. A drive that can take me twenty minutes to complete can take them hours just to get to their destination with their horse and buggy form of travel. That is a whole different mentality in living which must take patience modern lifestyles do not allow. So here I am. Like that yo-man antebellum farmer the product of the society I live in. A wasteful carbon emitting leech on the generations to come. My argument for changing my lifestyle and that of other "common people" lies in the same audience Greta Thunberg addressed. If you choose to be a leader of a society (either by free election or some other means) you have an obligation to exploit the best of what your society can do and needs to do for the future people who will live in it. Once something is recognized as dangerous to those outcomes, energies should directly flow in the direction to fixing the problem. Not toward an easier over-exploitation format which will not solve the problem. Too many times leadership will take the cowards path that history has shown leads to poor outcomes for "common people". Not for the elite. When the Confederacy was defeated in the Civil War it did not take the southern democrats anytime at all to regain substantial power. The graves of yo-men soldier who hit the wall at Gettysburg had not completely settled in the earth when former antebellum politicians were able to set up systems eventually to be known as "Separate But, Equal", or "Jim Crow" laws. Another example of elite resiliency lies in the Great Depression. In this economic disaster elite business owners sat on their money forcing the government to implement social programs that saved millions from homelessness, unemployment and malnutrition. After the Depression many of these elites gained huge profits off the post-war economic booms. In the case of climate change the formula will probably be the same.

Elite people can make decisions which hurt "common people" because the consequences for them are not as severe. In ancient China or Czarist Russia, the leaders had better make sure peasants had that "cabbage in their cabbage soup" or they could find themselves conquered and on a literal chopping block. In today's world elites have insulated their status so effectively that all would have to be lost for their lives to feel significant change. It does us well to realize we are talking about a very small group of people in comparison to the overall population. These people have means allowing them to move around the world comfortably. They can control many of the decisions from behind the scenes that "common people" get only glimpses of. So when a subject like climate change comes forward a lot of what is decided seems to go against information presented. How Can this happen? It happens because the elites simply would rather over-exploit what is increasing their wealth in the present time instead of making hard ,courageous , leadership decisions which would benefit everyone. They are banking on their ability to survive long term consequences of their actions and the confusion formulas provided by economic forces so sensitive to the lives of "common people". Statements like, climate change is a hoax. Or that the climate goes back and forth all the time and this is normal, kick the can down the road for more urgent and costly decisions to be made. Then there are the threats that "common people" would have regulations put against them making life even harder than it is now to make ends meet. Forced expenditures to update emission systems in cars and homes would cause pain and suffering to "common people" in their lives. Wait until the free market provides these items at reasonable costs for everyone and our emission problems will be solved. Like antebellum elites who defended slavery as the system benefited them and very few others, these elite climate deniers will milk the cow of over-exploitation until the cow dies. Then they will find a new cow. Greta Thunberg and her followers are trying to save our planet from these forces of over-exploitation. To many people it seems we are not making progress. Old men (and some women) sit in the seats of power without moving toward change. Change will eventually take place and the main hope for people like Greta is that the change is not the dire results of climate change.

The situation is not dire toward positive change and people like Greta can have hope (as do we all). The hope lies in our democratic systems that people simply have to take back through the peaceful means of the ballot box.

CHAPTER 15

THE CROSS IN FRONT OF THE VAMPIRE

Democracy was first devised by the Greeks on a societal scale. The system was very exclusive. Foreign people , slaves, and of course women (almost always left out in the ancient world) could not participate. Any Greek who had become impoverished enough to lose their property or have to sell themselves into slavery also could not vote. Even though this democracy seems exclusive by our standard, for the ancient world the idea of even an exclusive number of people ruling themselves was astounding. So astounding that not everyone in Greece bought into the system. Sparta developed a strict military state due to their over-exploitation of surrounding native peoples called Hellots. Their fear of uprisings by these enslaved people left freedom at the corner for the sake of security.

Athenians developed the first systematic democracy and for a while were the standard other states followed. In the Greek form of democratic rule all citizens belonged directly to the government in some capacity. As Athens grew this became somewhat cumbersome as some twenty thousand Greeks could be involved in direct decision making at one time. Still this idea that people could rule themselves without an overall tyrant was truly revolutionary. Even more revolutionary was the fact that it worked. Athens thrived. This exclusive group of Greeks choosing their own destinies provided all the incentives Adam Smith, Milton Freidman, and Alan Greenspan envisioned for our society as people followed their own self-interests. Warriors deciding when they would fight fought harder, business people deciding their own trade and market laws became more profitable, and, farmers making their own informed decisions about harvest and taxation grew surpluses of food most people benefited from. Soon other Greek city-states copied Athenian ways and Greece became the lantern for democratic rule in the ancient world.

The Greeks became highly educated. Greek liberal education ideals are still used today with the belief of creating the well informed citizen. Their studies of Philosophy, Geography, and medical science are foundations for learning twenty five hundred years later. With names like Socrates, Plato , and Aristotle being the results of a Greek education ,it showed how brilliant the trained human mind can become.

They developed into great warriors. The city-state (or Polis) was to be defended with a new vigor because people were fighting for their own freedoms. Greek military formations (known as phalanxes) relied heavily on teamwork and dedication to each other's chances for success and survival. The tightly packed ,heavily armored formations that needed to stay together for the victory and survival are a reflection of the Greek Polis and it's mentality. As a Greek you were a free person but, you needed to work effectively with others to survive and be successful.

These military tactics sprung from their democratic societal beliefs. Greeks did not have a constitution to provide a format for their government. It wasn't because they could not have thought of one, it was because the format for Greek society was to be in the minds of the people. No Greek male citizen raised in Greek educational ideals would purposefully make a decision that would hurt the Polis. An Athenian would do what was best for Athens. An Arcadian would do what was best for Arcadia. This was the argument to limiting the voting. People who were uneducated or incapable of making informed decisions would threaten society and make a government based on democratic principles to volatile to survive. Seasoned citizens who owned land and had fought to defend it would steer the best course for the Polis and it's success. For a long while this worked. Greek Polis's fought off tyranny both externally and internally and became the envy of the ancient world for success. It was not to last.

Many Greek Poli's (including Athens) began to fall more and more under the control of upper class elites. These people developed oligarchic rule which focused self-interest in a direction not advantageous for their society but, fitting the self-interest of those in power. Ill advised wars, poor trade systems, and a stubborn refusal to change in the face of adversity all helped to bring the Greeks to their knees. King Philip of Macedonia was able to exploit these weaknesses and take over the Aegean. He left the Spartans to their own isolated troubles yet he brought most of democratic Greece under his control. By the time of his assassination only the freedom loving Thebeians were holding onto democracy. They would get the ancient world version of a nuclear bomb for their mutinous ways by Philip's son Alexander. Why did Alexander (later Alexander the Great) need to destroy this Polis above all others? Athenians, not Thebeians had assassinated his father. Why would a despot fear this Polis more than the others. The answer lies in the Thebeians themselves.

The Thebeians were the last holdouts to true Greek democracy. They were for the most part farmers. They often voted down going to war and any leader that wanted to take these people away from their beloved land for anytime at all better have a good reason to do so. While people in Athens may have grown a little soft from the easier life of trade and business. Thebeians were hardened by their training and their livelihoods at the same time. When they united and went to war the resume of this freedom loving society was impressive to say the least. On that resume is the only true defeat of a fully manned Spartan Army. What made Thebians so lethal in war was what had made all of early Greece so tough. They went to war mad as hell that this inconvenience had been laid at their doorstep and they fought like crazy to end it quickly and get themselves home. Much like soldiers in the U.S. military during WWII, these Thebian men were semi-professionals who fought with an urgency difficult for tyrannical armies to copy. Thebian armies on the march were a fearful site and one not many opponents could defeat successfully. The fact was this marching did not happen too often. As I said before they did not like to go to war. Leaders had to really convince the "common people" it was in their best interest to go. Alexander realized to have Thebes in his kingdom meant continual danger of ticking off these very lethal citizen warriors. He handled them by destroying their Polis completely before they could form up against his military and threaten his rule. Thebes was the only Polis he destroyed this way. It is one of the ancient worlds best examples of a tyrant fearing the power of free people so much that he completely annihilated them.

The lesson of Greek failure to keep their democracy comes not from allowing Philip and then Alexander to take it away. The lesson lies in what happens when "common people" lose the decision making power of their society. The Thebeians are an example of the forces unleashed when "common people" are the main way decisions are made. In the case of Thebes it was when they went to war. Their successes in farming and holding their Polis together are less dramatic to historical record but, during a thebeian farmers lifetime was the most important thing to him. The Thebes of ancient Greece was a simpler time. To satisfy Thebeian farmers you need only let them farm. The "cabbage in their cabbage soup" was good fertile land to work and protect. They held their leaders accountable and for the most part their leaders delivered.

Which system do we want to be? Thebes or the rest of Greece. Our founders were true Thebeians. The British would find that these rag tag farmers (with training) could become as lethal as any force in Europe. Free thinking people have energies inside them that direct toward their best interests and make societies they live in armor plated against over-exploitation. History seems to teach us that the erosion of freedom's armor comes from within. That elite sectors of free societies can obtain unreasonable influences in decision making powers which neuter the energies of freedom. The self-interest of "common people" when used by Thebeian type societies where the elites are legitimately held accountable by the "common people", establishes fertility in progress and armor plating against over-exploitation by others. Legitimate democratic rule. Free of manipulating confusion formulas by elite classes can prevail over issues like climate change, terrorists threats, or periodic economic downturns. Like the Greek phalanxes of old, our society can protect itself. Our society can then open our armor exterior and help other societies reach levels greater than they have known due to the forces unleashed by these free environments for human development. Unexploited decision making by "common people" to better their lives is a key to defeating over-exploitation.

Unlike the Greeks our founders were wise enough to give us a format to follow. Our constitution is the framework to defend against what happened to the Greeks. The Constitution is designed with over-exploitation in mind. For it is the power and where it goes that determines how a society treats it s people. The Constitution is designed to keep power in the hands of the people.

The reasons for this are in the title of this chapter. Power is the blood flow for decision making. If the power is kept with "common people', the flow of blood through the body politic is even and healthy. When elites in society get unreasonable control of power through economic , political, or social influences, they grow the fangs of over-exploitation. Following their own self-interests they sink these fangs into the power blood of society and have an unreasonable and out of balance control over people. Like the mythological victims in a horror movie the "common people' fall prey to this power drain from their existence and can be led around to their doom by those controlling the flow of power. Our constitution is set-up to protect against this scenario. The Constitution is the Cross in the face of the vampire.

The problem is it cannot do it by itself. I use to tell my students it is just a piece of parchment. If "common people" do not enforce the words you might as well blow your nose with it. The hope that Greta Thunberg and the rest of us have lies in what Greta and her followers have done. Use your right to speak out (however you can) and hold those in power to the promises of freedom in the documents framing our society. Unlike the Greeks who relied on the mind-set of what it meant to be Greek. We have a document that says what freedom is and what it isn't. What power leaders can have and what power they cannot. The Greeks failed due to being human and over-exploiting their society from within. They came very close to doing it right. Hopefully we can finish the job for them and get it right this time. If not, there is not guarantee a chance at true freedom will happen again.

CHAPTER 16

TRUMP

I have used our current president in several examples in this book. The reason is fairly obvious. He is a true over-exploiter. He is a self-interested, "invisible hand", confusion formula, elite businessman who gained the reins of power by promising economically squeezed "common people" he could, "Make America Great Again". In this statement lies a ,Leave it To Beaver, "Ozzie and Harriet" type remembrance which is lily white and conveniently forgets that those images were not the best for everyone. Those people that do not benefit from his image of the United States are not the ones he is talking to. The white working and middle class people Trump speaks to are the same people Barrack Obama identified in his speech as frustrated by forces beyond their control. In 2016 they believed Trump could deliver and barely got him elected. What they elected to the highest office in our land is revealed daily in Tweets, turmoil, and temper tantrums creating a wild ride many Trump supporters enjoy. To many of these "Fifth Avenue" supporters of Trump (those who would support him even if he shot someone on fifth avenue) he is getting back for them a system they see as doing them no favors. They are not wrong in their analysis of these conditions. Although, their perspectives do not necessarily fit where the country is going.

The examples of this changing United States are everywhere. According to the United States Census one in every four newborns in the U.S. is Latino. Political maps of the southern United States show a growing and vibrant immigrant population that is motivated and will work at jobs Trump supporters do not want. LBGTQ Americans have gained more rights (including the right to marry in many states) which goes against many of Trump's evangelical supporters . Marijuana is becoming legalized. Certain gun models appear to be heading for the chopping block with the NRA now in financial and leadership crisis. The United States of their grandfathers is disappearing before their eyes. What was this idyllic time we are trying to get back too?

After World War II the United States of America was the top country in the world. We were more powerful than any society had been or probably would ever be. We had a weapon of mass destruction that we had used against an unrelenting adversary to try and limit the casualties (that is at least what we told ourselves and historians have debated the use of the bomb ever since). We were the undisputed champion of industry. Almost everything was made in America. This of course was because the rest of the industrial world had been laid as flat as a pancake. Western Europe was in shambles. Japan was a burning ember (not just from the atomic bomb but also, from firebombing dozens of wooden Japanese cities killing millions of people). Then there was Russia and Eastern Europe. Both decimated by taking on the heart of the Nazi war machine. Russia had fifty percent of it's industrial capacity destroyed. To get the same result in our country you would have to destroy every city from New York to Chicago to comprehend the disaster that happened to the Russian people.

In these circumstances our factories worked at full capacity. For almost three decades strong unions and high factory outputs put people in their own homes gave them cars they drove and promised them pension packages they could count on. All of this was assured for free white male citizens. The wives of these males often got to go along for the ride. However, as divorce rates picked up many ex-wives found that their economic security left with their husbands. The work was solid but, not too overwhelming. Gone were the days of back breaking unsafe work which aged people before their time. "Thirty and out" was the call for a worker at an auto factory and many manufacturers followed. So a worker could see thirty years of labor and hopefully a long (if he wasn't a smoker) and pleasant retirement.

Politically things seemed simpler. "Give'm Hell Harry" and "I Like Ike" seemed to be better days. So much was this image that a very successful T.V. series with the name "Happy Days" was made from this period of time. The promise that came out of this time period was that life could be good if you worked at it. Your kids would have a better life than you did and your life in the present was better than anyone's on earth.

Somehow this image forgets the Civil Rights movements that started in the 1950s. This image also leaves out southern lynchings of African Americans and their escape north in the "Great Migration". This time was not good for women either. As we already stated, low pay , sexual harassment, and lack of opportunities were all part of a woman's life during these golden times. These realistic remembrances are seen as un-patriotic by Trump and his supporters. Like those people wanting to remove con-federate monuments from public parks and boulevards, Trump supporters cry out,"what is wrong with them". "Can't they just remember the good old days".

This use of memory is all part of the confusion formula Trump and his loyalists put on the public. The word "again" in his slogan implies we were really good at one point but, all these tree hugging people who welcomed illegal immigrants into our country to take good jobs away while threatening the security of our altars, and fire-sides are responsible for Americas downfall. The message resonates with these people in a frustrating realization that it is easier for them to believe than the truth of what has happened to them and the society they want to live in. The rest of the world caught up to us, and while we were enjoying two week vacations and retiring after thirty years on the job , they went old school and over-exploited cheap labor to build basic factory systems. Usually these basic factories were textile driven and eventually replaced our textile industry. I remember in the 1970s Bob Hope (the famous come-dian) was the spokesman for an advertising campaign asking American consumers to "Look for the Union Label" They even had a song. It went like this:

> *Look for the union label*
> *When you are buying a coat, dress or blouse.*
> *Remember somewhere our union's sewing*
> *our wages going to feed the kids and run the house,*
> *We work hard but who's complaining.*
> *Thanks to the I.L.G. we're paying our way.*
> *So, always look for the union label,*
> *it says we're able*
> *to make it in the U.S.A.*

Even with the prestige of Bob Hope the campaign could not overcome the drive of companies and consumers to follow their self-interest and buy clothing made in places where union label workers could not compete. The same story would happen to the makers of batteries, watches, T.Vs, stereos and the list goes on and on. The best intentions to "Buy American" seemed to always run into the realities of expense and living within a system that gives just enough to make it. Life in a consumer society made the decisions for ever present unexpected expenses that caused belt tightening beyond normal planning. Of course the best insulator to this problematic existence is added training and higher levels of income. The problem for many people of my generation was the transition from our father's society with plentiful jobs good pay and excellent pensions to the more technical society that demanded this higher level of training. .

People who believed a High School diploma was all the education they would need found themselves unqualified for skilled jobs as the less technical manufacturing jobs either disappeared or were downwaged to unmanageable levels. The squeeze on incomes attracted them toward outsourced products which further alienated the United States worker from manufacturing tangible products. The question came, "does America make anything anymore"? All of these problems hit the "common people" too quickly for their financial situations to adjust without help. . They weren't willing to accept the fact that the road was going to be harder for them than it was for their fathers and grandfathers. As a result they tried to follow their parent's formulas of High School and then a good paying job . They got caught (as happens so often in the development of societies) between the good times and the changing times. When all of this combined on them they lashed out looking for reasons why life wasn't working out. Trumps "Fifth Avenue", supporters are looking for an America which will never come back to them. Their biggest blame lies in their unwillingness to see the truth.

What they are not to be blamed for is over-exploitation formulas which enriched elites while making the road for "common people" more difficult than it already is to navigate. These formulas are all based on short term profits with little if no chance for sustainable long term outcomes. The negative results are plain to see. If the American worker is replaced by outsourcing and robotics, who will be the consumers available to buy American products? A person with limited resources can only buy so much and what they buy is basic to their needs. The attempts to extend the "common person's" spending power have been strained to the breaking point making many corporations look for consumers outside the United States. Not only are workers being outsourced so are the consumers. The bottom line to all of this corporate profiting following the "invisible hand" is the American "common person" was not taken care of by the very system they supported for so long. The large corporations followed their own self-interests and stomped over the backs of their fellow countrymen. The "invisible hand" directed them to where the profits were but, not to where the betterment of the American society was located. They made huge profits for decades as 'common people" tried to keep up with dollar stretching strategies. Tactics such as: women entering the workforce to provide dual incomes for households.,men and women extending their hours at work until our society was working longer and harder than any society on earth, and finally using the equity on their homes as revolving credit to extend buying power which blew up in all our faces in 2008.

Trump is the answer "common people" in the white community turned to because he appeals to their deep beliefs in our society. He is one of them in a billionaire suit. He is brash, he is unapologetic , and gives the appearance of self-reliance. He is a white man that wants the white guy economy back. He says what they want said about our society and where it is going. Even if his promises are false and unrealistic it is what they want to hear will be done. If Trump fails to deliver it is the fault of the liberal unpatriotic outsiders who do not know what makes America great. . For these frustrated Trump supporters, Trump is a walking symbol of the Confederate Flag. He is a Merle Haggard song come to life. He is the living version of the middle finger to all those politically correct politicians that seem to talk above the heads of "Fifth Avenue" Trump supporters. This was a stigma people like Jeb Bush and Hillary Clinton could not shake when trying to run against him. Like a cheap bottle of bourbon, Trump will temporarily take away the problems faced by this portion of our society. The hangovers they experience are all over the news, dropping commodity prices for farmers, wild rides in stock exchanges , southern border walls funded and unfunded, and the never ending gaffs on twitter and in interviews. Yet, they continue to drink from his bottle of toxic rhetoric because it makes them feel better. Someone is finally speaking for them. What elites who can't stand Trump do not understand is they created Trump. When Bill Clinton and other liberal politicians allowed economic formats based on Alan Greenspan's "invisible hand" policies that did not include enhancing the lives of hard working "common people", the results in a free society were an outcry to George W. Bush and later Donald Trump. The "cabbage in the cabbage soup" requires more sophisticated outcomes in a society where "common people" have a say. Both political ideologies lost track of this in the last forty years of economic development. Even Barrack Obama could not repair the damages.

What can be learned from the rise of Trump is the need to take care of the "common people" in decision making. Sitting at a table with other elites to make decisions on the social ,political, or economic stages in our country should have first and foremost on it's agenda the support for the "common person". Their abilities need to be exploited. There is no question about that. Their exploitation is how our society drives forward for both elites and "common people". No single institution has shown more understanding of this necessity than our American Military. They have become the most lethal force on earth by following an exploitation model and not over-exploiting the men and women who fight in their ranks. They have shown you can change the system around and it is not an inevitable outcome with no hope for improvements.

CHAPTER 17

OUR MILITARY (BECOMING MORE THEBIAN THAN ROMAN)

In the history of the United States there are few examples to match the over-exploitation of Vietnam veterans and the lessons learned from that horrible experience. They are hopefully lessons that will never be unlearned by our military. The over-exploitation of combat veterans during and after the Vietnam War was a national disgrace. Sending young men into harms way without the necessary sophisticated planning required for limited military actions became an over-exploitation adventure the rest of the world watched in amazement. Revealing documents (such as the Pentagon Papers) told the sad tale of political and military leadership more worried about personal standing and reputations than lives lost in an ill-advised conflict.

The answer to the continued frustrations in Vietnam became more troops. Not National Guards called up to increase the manpower (those were the sons and daughters of the elites fulfilling their military service safely at home) instead use the "common people" without the connections or understanding to avoid the draft. Many of these "common people" went willingly and to be accurate only a small percentage of them saw combat. However, those who were put into the jungles, rice patties and sometimes cities of Vietnam would experience military planning that can only be explained through the willingness to over-exploit their very lives as soldiers.

The main tactic that evolved in Vietnam was called "search and destroy". The plan was to have our soldiers (usually Marines) walk through the jungle along the DMZ (Demilitarized Zone) or rice patties in the Mekong Delta of South Vietnam and see if they got shot at. Once they received fire they were to call in artillery and airstrikes on top of their positions so they could destroy the enemy in large numbers with superior firepower. To be the bait on a hook makes a poor impression for the shark who wants to eat you (not to mention all the feelings a person develops being bait). Many of the people used in this way realize quickly that they were expendable. What changes in the mind of a young person who feels expendable can travel down many mental paths. Some very dark and horrible, others very fatalistic and accepting. All of them put in this position to achieve higher body counts so we could kill so many Vietnamese they would reach a point of no return. That is to say we could kill more of their troops then they could recruit or replace in the battlefield. The key to this strategy was to kill their way out of the war. Expose numbers of our own troops in engaging the enemy while we would rain hell down on them with the sophisticated firepower our modern military commanded.

The problem was the enemy did not play along. They learned quickly that to take on the United States military in open combat was a losing strategy. They began to use tactics that were insurgency based or what are most commonly called guerrilla warfare. Hit and run methods which frustrated the idea of massive engagements and body counts. Digging tunnels underground to get away from the artillery and airstrikes were methods both Viet Cong (guerrilla insurgency forces) and the NVA (National Vietnamese Army) started using against United States forces. The most revealing technique of how tenacious the Vietnamese were in fighting was the use of the "belt buckle" tactic. Vietnamese military leaders told their men to hold onto the belt buckle of the soldiers they were fighting so if artillery and air power was called in they will kill their own people. This tactic adopted by the Vietnamese often led to in close small arms fighting that could create high casualties on both sides.

Fighting an enemy this determined and tenacious needed an honest all hands on deck approach to win any version of victory that would make use and loss of American lives legitimate in both practical and moral terms. Instead career minded leaders in both the military and the government tried to hide the realities of war on the ground with confusion formulas aimed at giving the best possible outlooks while trying to increase troop deployments in ways not alarming to the American public. The problem with this strategy is the same one governor Walker ran into with the roads. Like potholes in the road, you cannot effectively hide an American casualty. The confusion formula fails the smell test as "common people" with voting rights see many of their own coming home in body bags. Like the people of Thebes they want to know what is being fought for and it better be a good reason. The spinsters of information in this historic example were democrats. Robert McNamara and Lyndon Johnson tried to sell the war to Americans in a way that would make sense. They failed. They failed because the whole situation was set up for failure. Nobody who understood Southeast Asia believed their policies would work. None of our main allies agreed with what we were doing. All the information coming out of Vietnam pointed to failure. Desertions in the South Vietnamese Army were up. One repressive South Vietnamese government after another failed to win support of the "common people" and the attempts at weakening the enemy by killing so many of them they would give up seemed not to have worked.

What in the world were these people (who David Halberstam labeled "The Best and the Brightest" of their generation) doing formulating military and political policies that failed so miserably. There are many factors that go into this failure but, the reason they kept sending in more and more troops (until we had half a million people stationed in Vietnam) and used horrible tactics like "Search and Destroy", was because like Lee at Gettysburg they fell down the rabbit hole of over-exploitation of the "common people".

Johnson was suppose to be a man of the people. A democratic leader with a populist social agenda. He was for civil rights, better schools, medicare, medicaid, and increased programs for environmental protection. He dropped the poverty level in the United States from twenty two percent to eleven percent in four years. He labeled his programs the "Great Society". Within those same domestic programs he declared a "War on Poverty". How could he send so many American boys (and some girls) to this horror show of a foreign policy.

The Tonkin Gulf Resolution (often referred to as the "blank check") helps give the answer. This Act of Congress was passed in 1964 due to a questionable naval engagement between North Vietnam's tiny Navy and two of our naval destroyers. Nobody was killed or wounded in a confusing (and as it turns out) wrongfully analyzed crisis. The later investigations found one bullet had hit a U.S. destroyer named the Maddox. Johnson jumped on this incident to have congress give away the responsibility of to make sure Johnson did not over-exploit his powers or the people effected by them. Johnson was able to escalate troop levels through the draft or any other method he saw fit to defend American interest around the world without congressional approval. An unprecedented power that Franklin Roosevelt himself did not have during WWII. At first Johnson refused to use these incredible powers. In fact he held out for almost two years. Then the failed programs continued to be in trouble and the generals under his command began to ask for more and more troops. He eventually caved into the failing military situation he faced in Vietnam by sending in larger troop deployments asked for by military leaders equally frustrated with their inability to crack the Vietnam nut. The added troop deployments had temporary fixes and would eventually need more support. By 1969 the United States had five hundred thousand troops in Vietnam. Not all of them combat troops but, a lot more of them in direct combat than in 1964. Vietnam became Johnson's signature event during his presidency and his signature failure. He would not run again for the presidency in 1968 and would die on his Texas ranch five years later a somewhat haunted and tortured man for the over-exploitation practices he fell into during Vietnam.

Johnson was brash and unpolished as a leader. He often rubbed people the wrong way with his cultural back country Texas warts unapologetically exposed for everyone to see. He used the tactics of a playground bully to get his way and would often humiliate his staff in front of others just to show his authority. Yet, for all of this, the man had a heart. He was not a cold blooded unfeeling retch. His weakness was to look at the numbers more than the people he was using to achieve outcomes so poorly conceived. Once the casualty rates started jumping he should have halted the "Search and Destroy" tactics as not proportional to the objectives we were trying to achieve. That is why the founders made a civilian the Commander and Chief. Military people are trained to be aggressive. They are often like police dogs in their operations. Tranquil and calm during times of peace but, give them the command and their teeth come out ready to defend or attack whatever the mission calls for. Once they are unleashed there was a tendency (especially in Vietnam) to call for more military might as an answer to the unforeseen problems of engaging a very stubborn and adaptive enemy. The fact that Johnson caved to these demands in the face of failed tactics, willingly throwing United States soldiers into situations they had very little chance of succeeding at ,is the highest form of over-exploitation. He simply saw his own ambitions as leader of the United States as more important than the men and women he sent into combat. Congress eventually would stop this madness. After Watergate and the failed ability of the South Vietnamese government to hold together, we cut ties with South Vietnam and the image of the last helicopter leaving our embassy is burned into American historical memory as one of our greatest foreign policy failures.

The over-exploitation of Vietnam soldiers did not stop with the end of the war. Many of them had become opponents of the war on their return home. As time drug on it became very clear that Vietnam had over-exploited the "common people" who fought in it only to fulfill the ambitions of elite people wanting to establish United States dominance in parts of the world that saw our actions as old-time colonial dominance. Even more frustrating was the release of government documents showing they knew the policies were failures but, kept sending people to these highly dangerous environments just so they did not look weakened by failure. Then the most frustrating part of the whole insane episode began to leak into Vietnam's sad story. That somehow, these young men and women who had gone to Vietnam and put their lives on the line when (their lives were worth the most) were to blame for the outcome. The stories ran of them being on drugs. That officers lost control of troops. That soldiers were more concerned with wearing peace symbols on their helmets than putting bullets in their guns. That at times they had shown cowardice in combat and unlike former generations who defeated militarists Japan and Nazi Germany, these hippie soldiers were not up to the task.

The facts just don't support these statements and the good news is that almost all of these accusations have been rebuked over time. Yet, for a while Vietnam Vets had to wear that stigma. They were spat on when they got home as baby killers and often hid (in semi-shame) the service they had done for their country. I have heard stories of soldiers who knew each other for years as neighbors in civilian life without realizing both had served in Vietnam. Reunions of fighting units in many cases did not start taking place until decades after the war. The over-exploitation they experienced on multiple levels took years to heal and for some never really healed. The PTSD programs existing for the veterans of Iraq and Afghanistan did not exist for Vietnam veterans and many of them became casualties of this over-exploitative war by their own hand.

I remember the first time I really understood Vietnam was a bad place. In the neighborhood where I lived in Cedar Falls Iowa there was a small mom and pop grocery store that I could go to as a kid and buy penny gum with whatever money I found in the sofa or the floors I swept as part of my daily chores. Inside the store was a darkly oak stained display counter with a roll top glass cover that allowed customers to see the different displays of candy bars, potato chips and of course penny gum that my brother and I would go to buy. A customer could grab the wooden handle secured to the bottom trim on the cover and roll the glass up to pick out whatever item you wanted to buy. The place was right out of a Norman Rockwell painting. Many times behind the counter to take both my and my brother's penny was a teenage boy wearing a tattered letter jacket who was the son of the family that owned this store. He always seemed anxious to get these little rug rats out of the store so he could get back to cleaning the place and be done with his work. I would often times see this young man sweeping the sidewalk, washing the windows, and stocking the shelves at my favorite place to go and feed my overactive sweet tooth. Then one day I went to the store and it was closed. I had not seen the young boy for sometime. The father had taken up sweeping, cleaning, and stocking while my young mind had selfishly not asked where the young man in the well worn letter jacket had gone. I went to my mother and told her the neighborhood store was closed and it looked like nobody was in there. My mother looked at me sternly and said to stay away from the store and not to bother people who came out of there. I asked her why and she said that the people who ran the store got terrible news, that their son had been killed in

Vietnam. It was the first time I remember hearing, really hearing, the name Vietnam. The thing that bothered me the most, even as a little kid of six years old was that I did not even know his name.

There is some good news about the Vietnam experience. Many members of our military learned valuable lessons. They have displayed those lessons both in Iraq (another political debacle that could have easily over-exploited thousands of young Americans). You can see it in their tactics. As General David Petraeus said to reporters in one of his pointed briefings.,"You cannot kill your way out of an insurgency". He was willing and (eventually did) talk to members of insurgent forces who recently had fought against and killed United States soldiers. Petraeus created alliances that would end fighting on terms where the United States could at least stabilize conditions. He used our forces in carefully crafted operations that weakened enemy resistance while minimizing United States casualties. In short, he thought, "what would they have done in Vietnam?" and then often did the opposite.

As a result our military is a great example of how over-exploitation can be corrected. Instead of following the same format of over-exploiting people who are beneath your command to gain advantages at their expense. Your system changes to exploit people and their talents always remembering they are a valuable item you do not want to carelessly lose. Our military was more easily able to accomplish this very difficult change because they literately deal with life and death in their decisions. Like Lee at Gettysburg, they get to see the results of their mistakes as over-exploiters in all the horrific images of war. Seeing dead bodies of your own men after an ill-advised operation has a sobering effect that demands change. The reactions by a free society to over-exploitation can also jump start the temperamental engine of change. Negatively reacting free societies harm military effectiveness with low recruitment quotas and budget cuts from irritated politicians. War colleges quickly dust off books about limited operations with minimal casualties and forget the glories of all out victories by Patton and MacArthur. The lessons on massive military might are replaced with limited force combinations using troops and firepower in ways that limit casualties while maximizing results.

The process of exploiting the lethal abilities of United States forces in well planned operations creates a Thebeian type outcome to our use of force. The trade off to over-exploited military operations that anger American "common people" at the seemingly senseless loss of human life is long term commitments of United States forces with limited casualties. This trade off has worked simply because the over-exploitation element is taken out of the equation. The military is still a dangerous service. People unfortunately do get killed in operations. Yet, the Thebian ideals of reasonable and just operations of war approved by free people creates higher levels of support for future military operations and trust that human life is not just an unnamed number to be used without careful consideration. So a kid can become a young man and fulfill his own dreams with a tattered letter jacket on the back hanger in his closet next to an equally tattered military uniform.

CHAPTER 18

IS OVER-EXPLOITATION THE END?

There are many other examples of over-exploitation in our society. In the food industry the promoting through low prices and advertising campaigns have made sugar, corn syrup, and processed meats a regular part of the American diet. Is it any wonder we have an obesity problem when these types of foods are waved in people's faces night and day. Yet, overweight people are given the message that it is their choice to be heavy. Nobody forced them to eat these foods. Somehow they are suppose to navigate nutrition needs while keeping within the budget constraints demanded by ever decreasing incomes. When you can buy a dozen doughnuts for just over two bucks or a fast food burger for a dollar ninety five, it makes the buying of more expensive nutritional food much harder to do for cash strapped families. The hypocrisy of corporate sponsored politicians who push sugar through legislation but then, in the same halls of lawmaking try to limit nutritional programs for impoverished people while talking of "welfare queens" scamming the system would be comical if it was not so sinister in it s purpose. That purpose being to make money for elite owners off the subsidization of sugar and other mass food products while blaming poorer people through confusion formulas for the blight their over-all health is in. Then further the outrage by denying them universal healthcare.

Sometimes these over-exploitative models play out so plainly to me I wonder, does anyone else see what I am seeing?

Another area of horrific over-exploitation of "common people" is the opioid crisis. The information is still very fresh on how big pharmaceutical companies manipulated our markets to get thousands of people addicted to these pain killers. The evidence I have seen so far has all the makings of over-exploitation toward "common people' in order to make huge profits.

How many times does this pattern need repeating? Elite individuals with the ability to make tremendous amounts of money at the expense of "common people" will follow their own self-interests without the concern for outcomes to their fellow human beings. Adam Smith's ideals are based on meager profits made by small businesses closely tied to the community. Disconnected corporate giants often make decisions based on money and not people. To deregulate their activities into a human-made environment free of restriction cannot stop over-exploitation simply by reliance on the mythical powers of free market systems. Over-exploitation is the result due to the amount of potential wealth that can be obtained and the disconnection between decisions made and people effected. If people could make ten million dollars every time they ran a stop sign and then cover up their activity with a portion of the money they have made, nobody would ever stop at an intersection. We need our "common people" and social conscious elites to demand effective oversight of these companies to happen before the over-exploitation takes place. As I have expressed time and again we cannot achieve our "More Perfect Union" without their help.

These examples of over-exploitation can be found in other areas not totally related to the economic power given by great wealth. Often all that is needed is the ability for over-exploitation because of an environment where an elite is unregulated in dealing with others deemed lesser than themselves. I have already mentioned the "Me Too" movement revaluations which have come out in the past five years and how they changed ideals of women in the workplace. Another area that has been revealed in illegal over-exploitation is the Catholic Church scandals which have rocked that institution directly to it's core. Giving any human unchecked authority over others on a systematic scale has the makings for over-exploitation. Priests where often treated as living representatives of God. The unregulated authority priests had over people (especially children) created over-exploitation that often involved sexual abuse of victims. Priests are human beings. Give them unregulated authority and over=exploitation will occur no matter how deeply the mental and spiritual barriers to evil treatment of others might appear. The Church has taken many steps to change this system wide problem. Hopefully it can get back to it's original mission to care for people and fight against over-exploitation.

The good news is there are others looking to change our over-exploitative society.. I believe Barrack Obama was one of these people. I see people like Bernie Sanders and Elizabeth Warren also wade through the confusion models and try to expose them to the public. Indeed the comedian John Stewart made a career exposing these hypocritical formats in our society. They all seem to have fallen short so far in changing chronic over-exploitation. I believe two ingredients are needed by these leaders of "common people" to change the cycles of over-exploitation.

Number one is to get the elites to feel secure in their positions in society. In this I do not mean securing their wealth. I mean a campaign to recruit their energies toward exploiting the best our society can be without taking advantage of it in ways that threaten our very existence. I am glad to hear that many elite universities are adding morality and business responsibility courses to their business school curriculum. Hopefully these classes are teaching how great wealth demands great responsibility. Not just philanthropy but, decision making in business practices eyeing the future of our society's success. As I said before, elite people need to know their powerful influences and actions have consequences beyond the norm. Elite people cannot think that no matter what they try to accomplish in gaining profit that somehow it will have a positive effect on society. A rising tide does not raise all boats if you are throwing many of the boats onto the rocky shore.

To help guide their decisions there needs to be standard and agreed upon regulations which will prevent the human nature to over-exploit. Our government officials must develop these with elite people giving legitimate non over-exploitative input that will allow them to continue profit development and the drive to innovate better conditions for all people. This cannot happen if the "common people" are electing lawmakers who bow to over-exploiting profit seekers when they make decisions. Trying to be a person of the people while pleasing large political donors creates a hypocritical fuel that is the main source of energy for the confusion formulas allowing over-exploitation. Politicians continually trying to hide their support from big donors while telling "common people' they are in their corner, makes once very honest and truthful public servants lying and conniving shells of their former righteous selves. We need big money out of politics. Whichever future set of leaders who can accomplish this feat will remove the key ingredient to the recipe for our present confusion formula and over exploitation of the "Common people.

Number two is to get back to our better selves as "common people" and make our society of the 1950s and 1960s available to everyone. Good paying jobs with decent benefits so hard working people can have a good satisfying life. To do this in the modern world requires public education provided to the highest possible levels. White , Black, Latino, or Asian and the eventual combinations of all those categories of people need to have access to a fair shot at making their life a good one. We need to make our society a place where people can thrive to expose their best. I know it sounds, "Pie in the Sky" but, so does "A More Perfect Union" when you think about it. Human nature will always have people who achieve higher than others. Sometimes this is a matter of talent and will and sometimes it is a matter of choice. The choice can include not to be wealthy and work at an occupation that is fulfilling in ways other than wealth (teaching for example). If we create a society where reaching for wealth is the only measure of success worthy of reward then a lot of holes will be created that even elites cannot fulfill. I realize this perspective comes from a non-elite "common person" who worked in the public sector his whole life however, I really do not see any other way that will truly take our society forward.

In my lifetime I have seen parts of our nation improve. Rights for women and minorities are better than they once were. Treatment of LGBTQ students in schools is much better than when I was young and can still improve. The main area I have seen a true deterioration is how corporate America has followed their own self-interests in ways which leave "common people" with limited futures and less on the table than they once had. The economic elites in society saw opportunities to make gigantic profits without benefiting the very society which gave them the platform to reach such success. By buying politicians through campaign donations they solidified a confusing series of messages that could hide their activities of over-exploitation. They did follow Adam Smith's "invisible hand" and self-interest model yet, they did not follow his model on moral sediments.

How will history judge this period of time. Will the power elites in business and their supporters in Washington be seen on the same grounds as the emperors in China or of the Pharaohs of Egypt? Leaders who over-exploited their populations to build monuments to staggering wealth with no real benefit to society. I hope not. The main reason is that all those societies are extinct. They fell due to the unbalanced weight of over-exploitation. Our society is to be based on freedom and equality under the law. Rare items even in today's world. It sickens me that our present president may have recently made a decision in Syria to help keep his profits safe in Turkey while condemning a former trusted ally (the Kurdish people) to tyranny and loss of their freedom. This cannot be who we are. Sell out over-exploited people just for a few extra dollars. Our country should be a beacon, it should be the light in a potentially very dark world. I would hate to think freedom might die just so people could make a few more dollars. To say the "invisible hand" and self-interest is the key to our future development seems to condemn our society to more of the same over-exploitation. Following the unregulated free market format we have lost our way toward that "More Perfect Union". I do not believe many of the great leaders who helped build our society supported over-exploitation. I also do not believe they would look at a society where over 50% of the wealth is in the hands of a few elites while "common people" struggle to get by. The human shift toward a less greedy and selfish society sounds very Polly Anna and in its Utopian sounding ideals almost child-like. Very similar to the unrealistic beliefs of Karl Marx and Fredrick Engels. Yet, take a minute to realize how we got to this place of over-exploitation and egregious one-sided societal wealth. What caused it was a systematic change in how society structured and measured worth. For the past forty years our political system has supported big business and it's over-exploitation of "common people". Either to make short term gains in economic growth (like Ronald Reagan and George W. Bush) or out of necessary salvation from total economic collapse (like Barrack Obama). The point is we created this system. There is no such thing as a totally free market. The way the market is set-up is by people who wish it to work a certain way. We can set the free market up in such a way that over-exploitation is limited and rare and at the same time preserve the precious self-reliance of free markets. We just need to work on it together. So many things in a free society require people cooperating for it to work. Social media, the internet, stop signs at intersections , and our everyday courtesies that keep us from slamming doors in each others faces. All of these help us stay free from regulation and control. Keeping freedom and self-reliance are important for the United States. The product of that freedom should not be a form of slavery by wealth.

Chloe Anthony Wofford Morrison was one of our nations best novelists. When she taught her college course she ended them telling her students that if there was a book you felt has not been written then it is up to you to write it. So I wrote this book. It is an editorial inspired by the life of my mother. A woman who was over-exploited in her life but at the end felt good enough about it to call her existence on earth a positive adventure. My concern for society is that more and more people will not be able to say those things about their lives. Feeling the over-exploitation around them and the seemingly false promises of equality in life will create a society of people who will not be able to say ,"I loved what I did". My hope is that the few people who read this book may begin to understand what is happening and try to change it in their own way. If not than at least in this capacity I have fulfilled Ms Morrison's call. I wrote a book.